Reading, Learning and Media Education

Edited by Frank Potter

Blackwell Education

46912

First published 1990

Published by
Basil Blackwell Ltd
108 Cowley Road
Oxford
OX4 1JF
England

British Library Cataloguing in Publication Data
Reading, learning and media education.
   1. Education. Role of mass media
   I. Potter, Frank II. United Kingdom Reading Association 371.33

   ISBN 0–631–17754–X

Typeset in 11/13 pt Plantin
by Graphicraft Typesetters Ltd., Hong Kong
Printed in Great Britain
by TJ Press Ltd, Cornwall

Contents

iv *Reading, Learning and Media Education*

Preface

This volume contains a selection of the presentations given at the 1989 United Kingdom Reading Association Conference. I should like to take this opportunity to thank all those who helped to make the conference such a success, and I am only sorry that the restrictions of space made it impossible to publish all the articles. I hope that they will be published elsewhere.

To help readers find their way around this volume there is a brief description of each article presented below in list form. In addition a personal view of how the articles address two important issues can be found in the introduction, entitled 'Dimensions to literacy'.

Reading, communication, games Barrie Jacobs provides an analysis to help us avoid being trapped by the language we use. He points out that just because we refer to widely different activities as 'reading' this does not mean to say that they necessarily have anything in common. He proposes a 'games' metaphor as an alternative, more productive, conceptualisation – games in this context being social activities with their own rules.

New developments in media education Cary Bazalgette clarifies the relationship between media education and literacy, by making the distinction between print literacy and audio-visual literacy, discussing the link between the two, and subsuming both under media education. She also provides a framework for integrating media education into the primary curriculum.

Context, continuity and communication in learning Neil Mercer discusses some recent research into communication in learning in order to take issue with those individualistic conceptions of how people learn (which continue to inform such educational practice) and suggests how teaching-and-learning can be better understood as a social, communicative process.

Representations of literacy in the media Peter Putnis explores the characteristic ways in which literacy is constructed in the media as a 'problem' and the ways in which the media both reflect and propagate typical representations of the issue, and discusses the implications for educationalists.

Language, communication and reading Asher Cashdan argues that education is essentially a matter of communication, a two-way process where pupils as well as teachers have access to the tools and structures of learning. This includes grammar in some form, though not offered in such a manner that pupils cannot internalise it (ie not as formal grammatical analysis).

Text-processing with the computer: the implications for literacy David Wray explains why he regards the issues of autonomy and control as central to the concept of literacy, and goes on to outline some of the features and benefits of text-processing with the computer, with particular emphasis on provisionality of text and the control which text-processing can give the writer.

We learn written language much as we learn spoken language This was the subject of a formal debate at the conference between Jeff Hynds (proposer) and John Bald (opposer). The debate continued even after the votes had been cast (see the comments in the introduction, 'Dimensions to literacy', for an explanation as to why the debate provoked such controversy). As a matter of interest the votes cast before and after were as follows (the extra four votes at the end of the debate probably being those of latecomers):

	For	*Against*	*Abstain*	*Difference*
Pre-Debate	66	53	17	+13
Post-Debate	77	42	21	+35

My problems with real reading Geoffrey Lewis accepts the value of the use of real books in the teaching of reading but argues that there are identifiable flaws in some of the argumentation used in support of such ideas – which restrict the usefulness of the approach, and impede the development of a unified approach to the process of reading. His paper suggests some solutions to this problem.

Literacy learning in a multiethnic primary school: an Ethnographic Study Rebecca Huss examines factors which contribute to children's success in early literacy learning within the classroom, home and community contexts. These factors include an interest in and reasons for literacy learning, a risk taking attitude and having family members actively involved in the children's literacy learning. The implications for classroom practice are also reviewed.

The different registers of texts across the curriculum and what some pupils have to say about them Alison Littlefair reports discussions with readers of different ages and abilities about pages taken from books across the curriculum, which suggest very different degrees of pupil awareness, and concludes that all teachers need to help children develop their understanding of the different genres of subject texts.

Open learning – an introductory perspective Bruce Gillham moves tentatively towards a definition of 'open learning' by concentrating on those factors which seem to result in a closure of educational opportunity, and then reflects on the sorts of open systems which can overcome them. Open learning is seen as part of a much broader educational movement concerned with the nature of education and the problems of individual access to its benefits.

Open learning and basic skills provision for adults Gill Dempsey looks at the national context for the development of open learning within basic skills provision for adults, and then focuses on the experience of one of the newly established centres, looking particularly at the setting-up phase, use of technology and assessment/evaluation of progress.

Open learning and teacher education John Merritt argues that the need for a more open approach to learning in teacher education has become increasingly apparent in recent years, and goes on to describe an approach which is designed to make open education for teachers both professionally attractive and more widely accepted, with a particular focus on English and the Whole School Curriculum.

GCSE media studies – the way forward? David Davies reviews the progress made to date in the study of the media in schools, examines some of the key concepts of GCSE media education within the context of the National Curriculum, and suggests possible strategies for the future of media studies, one of which being that the media can be taught through English.

Newspapers in education Richard Beamish offers a number of practical activities to provide a starting point for using newspapers as a live resource appropriate to the needs of teachers and their pupils. The activities chosen are suitable for teachers themselves to use in a workshop situation.

The language of advertising Norma Mudd describes how she introduced the language of advertising to a group of 9–11 year old children, and discusses how advertisements from a wide variety of sources can help them choose and use a style of language (register) which is appropriate for their purpose. Also via advertising children may be introduced 'naturally' to some of the technical terms of their language.

Writers and readers: what do they know? An analysis of six stories written by and for children Ann Browne examines six books written by eight-year-old writers for younger children, to discover the linguistic, narrative and inter-textual devices that children use when engaged in writing a book. One observation she makes is that the accompanying children's illustrations seem to complement and extend the text.

Strategies for involving young children in word processing Jane Medwell explores some organisational strategies for the development of word processing skills among young children, to help overcome some of the practical constraints of time, access and organisation which militate against effective use of word processors in the classroom. The use of peer tutoring is particularly stressed as a learning and teaching strategy.

Frank Potter

Acknowledgements

On behalf of the United Kingdom Reading Association, I should like to thank the following for their help in ensuring the success of the 1989 UKRA conference on 'Communication and Learning':

The Conference Committee, mainly composed of the Ormskirk Local Council: Liz Eccleston, Anne Hothersall, Shirley Fairnie, Caroline Jackson, Trine Kienstra, Beryl Malins, Donald Moyle, Daphne Mortimer, Norma Mudd, Pauline Richardson, Heather Sands, Angela Trotter, Steve Walker, and Judith Wright.

Hazel Clarke, the Administrative Secretary of UKRA.

Edge Hill College of Higher Education, and in particular Sue Claridge, the staff concerned with catering and accommodation, the porters, the computer unit, and the conference office.

The Educational Publishers' Association, particularly Ruth Stuart, Carol Edgecombe, all the exhibitors, and Madeleine Lindley.

The speakers and those who submitted papers for inclusion in this volume. Unfortunately limitations of space meant that not all the papers could be included. I hope those that had to be omitted will be published elsewhere.

Finally, a special thanks to Heather Sands for her invaluable help and support both before and during the conference.

A note on the contributors

Frank Potter is President of the United Kingdom Reading Association and a Senior Lecturer in Education at Edge Hill College of Higher Education, St Helens Road, Ormskirk, Lancashire.
Barrie Jacobs is a Senior Lecturer in Education at Edge Hill College of Higher Education, St Helens Road, Ormskirk, Lancashire.

Cary Bazalgette is Deputy Head of BFI Education at the British Film Institute, 21 Stephen Street, London.

Neil Mercer is Director of the Centre for Language and Communications at the Open University School of Education, Milton Keynes.

Peter Putnis is Associate Professor of Communication at Bond University, Queensland, Australia.

Asher Cashdan is Professor and Head of Department of Education at Sheffield City Polytechnic.

David Wray is Lecturer in Education at Exeter University.

Jeff Hynds is a freelance Lecturer and visiting tutor for INSET at the University of London Institute of Education.

John Bald is Tutor in charge at the County Language and Reading Centre, Colchester.

Geoffrey Lewis is a Lecturer in Education at Trent Nottingham Polytechnic.

Rebecca Huss is a Doctoral Student of Early Childhood Education at Georgia State University, Atlanta.

Alison Littlefair is a Consultant in Language in Education, 56 High Street, Harlton, Cambridge.

Bruce Gillham is a Principal Lecturer at Newcastle Polytechnic.

Gill Dempsey is a Field Consultant at the Adult Literacy and Basic Skills Unit, Kingsbourne House, 229–231 High Holborn, London.

John Merritt is Emeritus Professor at the Open University and Honorary Research Fellow at Charlotte Mason College of Education.

David Davies is Subject Officer for GCSE English and Media Studies, London East Anglian Group, Stewart House, 32 Russell Square, London.

Richard Beamish is Manager, Newspapers in Education, The Newspaper Society, Bloomsbury House, 74/77 Great Russell Square, London.

Norma Mudd is Lecturer in Communications, Southport College of Further Education, Southport.

Ann Browne is Lecturer in Language and Primary Education, West Sussex Institute of Higher Education, Upper Bognor Road, Bognor Regis.

Jane Medwell is Lecturer in Education, University of Wales College of Cardiff.

1 Introduction: dimensions to literacy

Frank Potter

The reader will find an outline of the contents of each article in the preface. Here a personal view is presented of how the articles can contribute to our thinking about two important 'dimensions' to literacy: the first concerning underlying philosophies of literacy teaching, the second concerning the relation of literacy to media education.

How should we help children become literate?

This fundamental issue was addressed directly or indirectly in very different ways at the conference, by Barrie Jacobs, Neil Mercer, Asher Cashdan, Rebecca Huss, Geoffrey Lewis, David Wray, Bruce Gillham and Peter Putnis, in addition to the debate between Jeff Hynds and John Bald over whether *we learn written language much as we learn spoken language*.

Whereas twenty years ago the controversy was over 'look-and-say' versus 'phonic' approaches, this has now been replaced by a new debate (or debates): meaning-based versus skills-based teaching approaches; 'top-down' versus 'bottom-up' methods; holistic versus subskill methods; real books versus reading schemes.

The assumption is sometimes made that the controversies are capable of empirical resolution, and that for example 'closer examination of what is known about spoken language acquisition may, in fact, reconcile the real books approach with that which advocates a more structured approach to the teaching of reading' (Lewis, this volume). To me this seems most unlikely. Empirical evidence is always relevant, but it is hard to believe that such passions can be aroused by matters capable of empirical resolution.

The vehemence of the debates seems to signal some deeper underlying disagreement and, as Barrie Jacobs observes, 'This debate is being conducted with passion, sometimes with acrimony, largely because the question is not really one of methods but of definition and the power to define will always be fiercely contested.'

Before we can tell what empirical evidence is even relevant we need some conceptual clarification of the issues. Barrie Jacobs' chapter gives us an excellent start. He points out that we are tempted to assume that all uses of the term 'reading' must have some element in common (an 'essence'). An alternative to this essentialist approach is one which characterises the similarities as 'family resemblances', and he goes on to explore how this conceptualisation can help us obtain a clearer understanding of language.

Another assumption that is sometimes made is that there is only one literacy and that it is a 'neutral' technology. Teaching literacy then simply becomes teaching a technical skill. The alternative to this conservative view is that literacy is a set of social practices and relations, and that literacy learning is learning particular roles, forms of interaction and ways of thinking, in which case there will be many literacies, depending on the social institutions in which they are embedded (Street, 1984). This alternative view is specifically mentioned in this volume by Neil Mercer, Jeff Hynds, Rebecca Huss and Peter Putnis, and seems to me to have much in common with Barrie Jacobs' metaphor of 'language games'.

For example, one of Rebecca Huss's conclusions is that 'Second language children often come with the perspective of the ways reading and writing are used in their culture, for religious purposes for example, and may need to be introduced to additional uses of literacy, such as for communication and enjoyment.' The connection with Alison Littlefair's work is obvious when she defines what is meant by a genre: 'In this sense genres are seen as the purposeful activities which make up the culture in which we live. She also quotes Kress as describing the aim of reading as providing access for all children to the cultural forms of the society in which they live.' As David Wray reminds us, another distinction is that made by Castell, Luke and Egan (1986) – the classification of literacy into elitist, functional and mastery views – and issues of autonomy and control are seen to emerge as central to the concept of literacy.

When one takes into account the different ways of conceptualising literacy it would perhaps be more surprising if we *did* all agree about how to help children become literate. The controversies provoke such passion because they have a political and philosophical base, and as Asher Cashdan says it is inevitable that within education there should be a political argument, as education *is* a political activity.

Peter Putnis's chapter should dispel any misconception that literacy is neutral. As he says, 'The literacy debate, as presented in the mass media, is dominated by images of decline and crisis. Literacy is not merely a necessary skill but an index of the health of society. In fact the literacy issue is the site upon which a myriad of personal and societal anxieties, prejudices and ideologies materialize and contest.'

It is only after we have defined our philosophical position that the empirical evidence and theoretical models become relevant. In the past there has been a 'stark, crude choice between the didactic, authoritarian pedagogy of traditional education and the discovery-led, 'invisible' pedagogy of high progressivism', as Neil Mercer phrases it. In his chapter he offers us a new 'communicative' perspective, which emphasises the building of a contextual framework of knowledge and understanding between teachers and learners, and the 'scaffolding' of learning through communication and interaction. He emphasises that it is important that 'through the communication, the knowledge and understanding comes to belong to the children', that 'there must be 'handover', so that the learners come to possess what they have learnt.'

For Asher Cashdan it is also important that teachers adopt approaches that 'liberate the learner to be in charge of their own learning processes'. For him part of this is knowledge of the ABC and grammar, but he argues that neither traditional direct teaching nor incidental learning in context guarantee success. Part of what does guarantee success is a 'genuine offer' which may or may not be taken up – which presupposes some element of control on the part of the learner. This element of control is of course part of the underlying philosophy of Open Learning. As Bruce Gillham comments, 'The whole business of 'making sense' has shifted from the bearer of authoritative messages to pupils and students. Learners are increasingly expected to construct their own realities from the information and ideas provided.' As Gill Dempsey points out,

'There is no room for the traditional active teacher/passive student role in an open learning situation.' John Merritt regards open learning as 'merely an extension of what we normally do in our own everyday lives – and an extension of the behaviour that led to our own development of competence in language development from an early age! When we view English teaching as the teaching of a variety of skills we look at language development through the wrong end of the telescope.'

Approaches which *impose a fixed structure* are the very antithesis to open learning – it is not so much whether the structure is there, whether it is offered, but whether an attempt is made to impose it. It is whether or not learners are given responsibility for their learning. The debate is a philosophical and political one, a question of different world views, and hence not capable of empirical resolution. If it were then it should be possible to ask what evidence would convince one side or another to change their point of view. I doubt if any of the evidence presented by either side is of this kind.

For example, a few years ago the meaning-based, holistic, 'top-down' proponents (for example Goodman and Smith) supported their argument by appealing to the then dominant view that fluent adult readers did not read 'word-by-word' let alone 'letter-by-letter' but by using the context to predict their way through the text, and only sampling the visual information. Over the past few years we have learned a lot more about the reading process and it is no longer thought that fluent adult readers use such a contextual predictive strategy. The accepted view now is that fluent adult readers read too quickly to be able to make a prediction on the basis of the context (Ellis, 1984; Mitchell, 1982). Yet I do not detect any weakening of the meaning-based position – if anything the opposite.

Rather than spending time searching for empirical evidence we should be clarifying the conceptual position. Is there one debate, or many? Is there one difference of opinion, or many? Are there two positions, or many? One dimension is that of the amount of choice and control one gives children. The important issue is not so much whether there is a reading scheme in the classroom, but whether children have a genuine choice about whether they use it or not. It is about whether they are given responsibility for using it, or whether they are dragged through it regardless.

Media education

Another dimension of literacy concerns its relation to other media. Recent government reports have specifically mentioned media education, but in such a way as to confuse rather than clarify the relationship between English/literacy and media education. This relationship is considered by David Davies, in which he discusses whether media education should be part of English, English part of media education, or both form part of a combined subject.

Cary Bazalgette clarifies the issues in her chapter 'New developments in media education'. She points out that as print is itself a medium, so 'anything that calls itself media education can't logically avoid addressing all media from books to satellite TV.' She suggests that we use the term 'media education' to embrace 'print literacy' and 'audio-visual' literacy. This analysis entails that print literacy is part of media education, and that what is sometimes referred to as media education should be renamed audio-visual literacy. In that case those of us concerned with print literacy will automatically be concerned with media education, but need we be concerned with audio-visual literacy? As Cary Bazalgette explains this depends upon which of three ways the link is made between audio-visual literacy and print literacy, whether one takes the conservative view that audio-visual literacy is simply a useful aid to learning and that print is the most important medium, whether one takes the radical view that they are essentially the same, or whether one takes a more cautious line, acknowledging the differences and arguing for more research into the links between them.

There is no doubt that audio-visual literacy is important. For example in the 1970s it was estimated that children of school age were spending more time watching television than at school (Masterman, 1985), and the *Guardian* (7 April 1989) reported that there were then more video shops in America than bookstores. The importance of audio-visual literacy has also been recognised by the Cox Report (14.13): 'Television now provides a significant proportion of the language experience of many children. It is therefore important that they understand better how words and pictures are used on television'. Indeed the 1989 Guardian Young Businessman (sic) of the year, Michael Green, would stand the conservative view on its head – he was quoted as saying 'Forget books. This is the age of videoliteracy' (*Guardian*, op cit).

It is clear that the 'conservative view' must be false, but whether one takes the radical or the cautious view may depend on what is meant by 'effectively the same'. Cary Bazalgette points out that the conceptual structure that can be applied to the study of audio-visual texts can also be applied to printed texts, so there are obvious fundamental similarities. But of course there are also differences, and Greenfield (1984) has pointed out that because of these differences, different media will find different niches. Print is the best medium for portraying thought, radio for stimulating the imagination and fostering creativity, and television for communicating feelings and promoting visual skills (Greenfield, op cit).

But even these differences mean that we need to consider print literacy in the context of other media literacies, as the appropriate niche for each medium is affected by which other media are available. As McLuhan said in 1964: 'A new medium is never an addition to an old one, nor does it leave the old one in peace.' Put another way, we can only really understand the functions and purposes of print literacy by understanding its role in relation to other media. As Berger remarks in relation to the meaning in texts (p 145): 'I believe that the bipolar oppositions that semiologists find in texts are actually there; not only that, but they *have* to be there. Finding meaning without discovering polar oppositions is like listening to the sound of one hand clapping'. Following Berger we might say: considering print literacy without considering other media literacies is like listening to the sound of one hand clapping.

Moreover, audio-visual literacy and print literacy are not compartmentalised in the real world, even in the publications of eight-year-old children, as can be seen in Anne Browne's contribution. One of her observations is that the children's illustrations seem to complement and extend the text, and that the pictures and the text work together to produce a more comprehensive detailed and clear story than is possible by the use of one medium on its own.

This natural complementary function of pictures and writing is sometimes denied by the practice of asking infants to draw a picture and then write a sentence duplicating the information in writing. As Maclure (1985) has pointed out, this must hinder children's appreciation of the communicative function of writing.

Such examples of children's early writing are essentially captions for their pictures, and the function of captions is to disambiguate the picture (or, to use the jargon, as images are polysemous, captions offer a 'preferred meaning' – see eg Gauthier, 1976). The competition for thinking of new captions for old Punch cartoons is a good example of this process at work (although here perhaps the trick is to suggest an unlikely meaning to the image).

The computer as a word or text processor is a tool for which we are gradually learning to find a niche: I have argued (Potter, 1988) that word processors are at present best used in schools for short, non-narrative, public texts produced collaboratively. Jane Medwell would broadly support this viewpoint: she recommends limiting the type of writing that is done on the word processor to writing intended for an audience other than the teacher and writer, collaborative writing, and tasks such as books for younger children, newspapers, reports of science work etc.

David Wray in a more speculative vein reflects on how this new medium may affect children's perceptions of literacy, and even the nature of literacy itself. His thesis is that text processors emphasise the provisionality of text, and give more control to the writer. Which brings us back to the philosophical questions mentioned in the first half of this introduction. How do we view the computer – as a threat to individuality, or as a new literacy tool which gives children more power and autonomy?

References

Berger, A. A. (1982) Semiological analysis. In Boyd-Barrett and Braham P. (eds) *Media, knowledge and power*. London: Croom Helm.

Buckingham, L. (1989) Green: stand by for TV's Euro explosion. *The Guardian*, Friday 7 April, 1989.

de Castell, S., Luke, A. and Egan, K. (1986) *Literacy, society and schooling*. Cambridge: Cambridge University Press.

Ellis, A. (1984) *Reading, writing and dyslexia*. London: Lawrence Erlbaum Associates.

Gauthier, G. (1976) *The semiology of the image*. London: British Film Institute.

Greenfield, P. M. (1984) *Mind and media: The effects of television, computers and video games*. London: Fontana.

McLuhan, M. (1964) *Understanding media*. London: Routledge Kegan Paul.

Maclure, M. (1985) *Early genres learned too well? Some comments on the first texts of beginning writers*. Paper presented at the International Writing Convention, held at the University of East Anglia, Norwich, April 1985.

Masterman, L. (1985) *Teaching the media*. London: Comedia.

Mitchell, D. C. (1982) *The process of reading*. Chichester: John Wiley and Sons.

Potter, F. N. (1988) *The word processor: a new literacy tool*. Paper presented at the European Community Summer University on 'Writing and First Contacts with Written Language' held at the University of Toulouse le Mirail, July 1988.

Street, B. V. (1984) *Literacy in theory and practice*. Cambridge: Cambridge University Press.

2 Reading, communication, games

Barrie Jacobs

Reading is in danger; reading is enjoying a revival; the nature of reading has changed so drastically that it is impossible to decide one way or another. Each of these positions has its adherents, and each is in some significant sense true (and in equally significant senses, false). We are said to be engaged in what is termed the new debate in reading (Wray, 1989) where the issue is not phonic vs whole word approaches, but reading as meaning making as opposed to reading as word identification. This debate is being conducted with passion, sometimes with acrimony, largely because the question is not really one of methods but of definition, and the power to define will always be fiercely contested.

There is, then, a logically prior question before we can start investigating how things are with reading. In recent years when this question of what is reading has been posed there has been a noticeable shift in both linguistic and social context. Instead of a relatively discrete bundle of skills, reading has come to be seen as 'literacy', with consequent emphasis on relationships between the reading and the writing of texts as social practices. Then the issue became 'whole language', the organic unity of language in its various modes. And a further real possibility is 'communication', where messages are encoded in symbol systems other than the purely, or even largely, verbal.

How can this extended context help us understand what reading is? One interesting possibility is that it might make it clear that there is something odd in the way the question is put. It is a simple fact about English (though it may turn out to be a hugely trivial fact) that we read things other than print such as palms or tea leaves. Then, people with newspapers read the news, and television newsreaders read the news, but they are clearly doing rather different things. In more academic terms, texts such as *Reading television* (Fiske and Hartley, 1978) and *Reading the screen* (Izod, 1984) are certainly not concerned with teletext. The idea that there is a range of phenomena that can be 'read' should come as no great surprise but the fact that different orders of events involve many different symbol systems may well mean that our skills in dealing with the verbal text (especially in its written form) may not simply lead us into misunderstanding, but of actually devaluing, other forms. As Gillham (1983) has noted, our literate perspective may well lead us to overstress elements which most closely resemble verbal dimensions within texts which are designed to work in a more iconic fashion.

The problem quite simply is that reading is not anything really (it is the 'really' that causes the trouble). In a significant sense, reading is what we say it is. There is no overwhelming fact about the natural world to be established by research and investigation. As a human activity reading is invented, not discovered, and in principle we have control over how we choose to describe our cultural inventions. Further, activity can be described from two points of view, that of the participants (what they see themselves as doing) and that of an observer (what the participants can be seen to be doing). Reading, then, is a matter both of eye movements and the like, and of comprehension and purpose. We must learn to avoid the rhetoric of either/or and explore the possibilities of at least/not only.

In short, the question is not about what reading is, but what we want it to be. What are our reasons for wanting it to be one sort of thing rather than another, and what are the consequences of one conceptualisation rather than another? If we take 'consequences' as the significant criterion it will not be too surprising that 'meaning' emerges as a central concern. But 'meaning' is itself a fuzzy concept and once more the temptation is to sidestep the issue and look for help in the extended context mentioned earlier, that of communication.

Perhaps the best known characterisation of a communication system is that of Lasswell (1948): 'who – says what – to whom – in what channel – to whom – with what effect', usefully supplemented by Braddock (1958) with 'under what circumstances – for what purposes'. Parallel with this line of work there had developed an engineering approach to communication, the work essentially of Shannon and Weaver (1949) who formulated a model of

Source – (Message) – Transmitter – (Signal) – Receiver – (Message) – Destination

Two points in particular must be noted. First, the actual meaning of the message is not the issue in the engineering approach ('information' in this context simply does not have the same meaning as in everyday language) and consequently the distinction between a message and a signal must be kept in mind – a signal is what is sent; a message is what is meant. Secondly, Shannon and Weaver are clear that a communication process presumes the existence of a set of messages shared by source and destination prior to transmission of any given signal. This suggests very strongly that, in the context in which we wish to use these ideas, questions over the degree of correspondence between the initial states of sources (writer) and destinations (reader) are central. The relevance of this to the work of Edwards and Mercer (1987) on the presence or absence of shared ground rules for classroom discourse is apparent.

With the addition of other central concepts covered in introductory texts (Fiske, 1982), noise (pseudo information generated from within the system), redundancy ('unnecessary' information included to compensate for what is obscured by noise) and most importantly, feedback (a source's knowledge of how effectively the process is working), we have the basis of a perspective for viewing and coming to a clearer understanding of what happens in an activity such as reading. The astute reader may, however, not be too happy with this confident assertion. If the original problem was the inability to define 'reading' adequately, a solution which depends on an equally undefined concept of communication seems less than adequate. Have we merely shifted the problem to a different level?

It is tempting to think of definition as the search for what something essentially is; there must be some common element (an 'essence') in all the instances, otherwise why would they all have the same name applied to them? An alternative to this essentialist approach does, however, exist. The philosopher Ludwig Wittgenstein in his later work, *the Battle to prevent the bewitchment of intelligence through language* (Wittgenstein, 1953), argued that while in some cases there is some central feature, an essence, such that possession of it qualifies as an instance and lack of that feature disqualifies (triangles, and the property of being a plane surface bounded by three straight lines, for example), the extent of this commonsense approach may be more limited than we imagine. Crucially, it should not be assumed that there is some essence; as Wittgenstein comments 'don't say there must be something in common ... but look and see' (para. 66).

The example Wittgenstein uses to illustrate the argument is 'games'; if we do actually look and see, it becomes clear that there is nothing in common to all the activities to which we apply the term. The range involved – board games, ball games, word games, etc – is merely the first point, for within any one of these categories the range of differences is equally wide. 'The result of this examination is, we see a complicated network of similarities overlapping and criss crossing' (para. 66). 'I can think of no better expression to characterise these similarities than "family resemblances"' (para. 67). When viewed as a collection of members, a family can be seen as displaying a pool of characteristics such that each member has some but not all, no two members need to have the same set, and indeed no two members need to share any single characteristic, nor does any single member have to have any particular characteristic at all.

In applying this family resemblance, rather than the alternative essentialist, model to language, Wittgenstein uses the term 'language games' to refer to the different sorts of activity which, through the network of overlapping relationships permeating social interaction, constitute the abstract whole we think of as language. The term 'game' does not carry the connotation of either frivolity or of being a matter of choice. In everyday terms games are in contrast to the serious business of life, while normally no one is under any obligation to participate in playing games at all. The metaphoric use in connection with the purpose activity of language involves a change. The choice is of which language game to play, not of 'doing language seriously'. At the most we can only opt out of language altogether (and even here, silence may well turn out to be a particularly subtle language game itself). We can play our language games seriously or not, but the fact that we are calling them games in no sense implies that they are trivial.

To adopt this model of language in preference to an essentialist one involves a change in our perception of language activity. The first task is not to judge utterances as correct or incorrect (or even appropriate or inappropriate) but to identify the language game in which they play a part. Issues of correctness and appropriateness are relative to the 'rules' of particular games. Secondly, in principle no one language game has priority over any other; informing is not necessarily better or worse than joking. Assumptions about the priority of particular games involve decisions often based on power rather than on appeal to the facts of language. Further, the list of language games is open and infinite. New members need not be examined for the mysterious essence but for how far and for what purpose we can fit them into the complex network of interrelationships involved in the games we currently play. Learning a language game is not just a question of learning 'rules', but of developing the ability to participate in the activity in which the 'rules' operate as limiting factors.

The fuzziness of some aspects of this approach only serves to underline the basic insight, that at every stage we are dealing with human decisions, not the reading off of facts about the natural world. 'Games' provides us with a metaphor, a way of thinking about a network of activity. The next step is to start delineating the specific activities that constitute the network. What games do we play, what games are there to be played?

A number of writers have already utilised the concept of games to explore aspects of experience in which we have a particular interest. At the level of everyday life, Berne (1964) spelled out the intricacies of interactional analysis in terms of what he called 'the games people play'. Classroom interaction has been analysed for us, notably in the work of Sinclair and Coulthard (1975), but the American research on which it is partly based is perhaps not so well known. In this Bellack et al (1966) give a detailed account of what they term 'the language game of teaching and learning', the complementary set of rules for teachers and pupils as players. A third example comes from the field of literature where, to explore the curious relationship between writer and reader, Hutchinson (1983) takes us through a substantial list of the games authors play.

A brief case study may help to illustrate the way in which some consideration of what game might be being played can help us understand the nature of a text. Prior to Kingman and Cox and the National Curriculum, a series of HMI documents designed to encourage debate by offering suggestions over the whole range of compulsory schooling had been produced. The first of these (DES, 1984) dealt with the subject of English. The natural response is to read it in terms of what it has to say about language in school. There is, however, some point in reading it in terms of the language game it plays in saying whatever it has to say about language. The form of the document is largely based on a distinction between objectives and other phases of the curriculum process. This approach borrows both the assumptions and the language of what has been termed the rational model of planning seen in its clearest form in the work of Bloom et al (1956) as a schematic, linear, deductive account of end products to be achieved through the process of education. As Davies (1976) has pointed out, the rational logical dimensions have their origin in earlier schools of scientific industrial management. The point is to reinforce an impression of compelling logic based on real objectivity.

The scientific character of the rational planning through behavioural objectives movement requires that objectives be phrased in a strictly limited language to guarantee precision. Thus, in the document under consideration, each section of age related objectives is introduced by 'at the age of . . . therefore, most children should be able to . . .', followed by a list of the specified behaviours. Understandably, most attention was devoted to the content of such lists, but we should not overlook the consequences of the style of the writing on our understanding of what is being argued.

One point can be dealt with fairly briefly – the function of 'therefore'. The normal use of this is to signal a conclusion, but there is a vast difference between a conclusion as the logically valid implication of a set of premises and as the summing up in brief of a set of arguable propositions. The tone of this format is designed to reinforce the alleged deductive nature of the conclusions.

More importantly, however, it can be shown that adherence to the particular rhetorical style produces some strange results, even what is in some cases literally nonsense. Bearing in mind that every objective is prefaced by the words 'most children should be able to . . .', we discover that:

1   'at age 7 most children should be able to know the alphabet.'
    Does this mean that they should actually know the alphabet,

or that they should merely be able to (whatever that might mean)?

2 'at age 11, most children should be able to know how to find books they need in a library'; the concept of 'being able to know how to . . .' (not just being able to or knowing how to) is a puzzle.

3 'at age 11, most children should be able to have some ability to adjust form, content and style of writing to nature of task and needs of reader'; 'being able to have some ability to . . .' is not simply puzzling, it is a good way down the path to the ultimate.

4 'at age 11, most children should be able to be able from a text to draw inferences'; by this stage no comments should be necessary.

It might be argued that these (and a substantial number of similar oddities) are simply curiosities of style, a by-product of the speed with which the paper was produced. This becomes less convincing when we notice that they reappear in the revised version of the document (DES, 1986). It becomes quite difficult to avoid the conclusion that the nonsense produced is a function of the rhetorical style adopted and that this style, a game that can be called 'schematic scientism', is often in evidence when it is necessary to generate a level of plausibility and logical compulsion for an audience that might otherwise exercise its critical faculties rather too carefully.

While it is true that the family resemblance concept allows us a wider view of what counts as 'reading', while still allowing us to acknowledge significant differences, it would be overstating the case to claim that a games approach is an answer to all our problems. It is merely a way in, and even as an approach there are some immediate notes of caution. There are at least three levels where the range of activity and the nature of the analysis involved might interfere with either our willingness or our ability to take it on. There is a level of background knowledge without which it becomes, if not impossible, at least difficult to understand the nature of games outside our conventional literate experience. The temptation to see visual media as unproblematic, as natural representations, does not only lead to our ignoring the technical dimensions involved but also to our blindness to the issue of intertextuality. It is not only written text which can depend for much of its meaning on our familiarity with a range of other similar text elements; makers of television commercials both obviously and more subtly pay homage to the world of the cinema. Do we or our pupils have at present the same range of experience of non-literary as we have with traditional text?

At the level of skills, it can be argued that while different media may virtually converge in terms of message, they diverge in terms of the skills required for reading the message, and the skills developed by reading messages of that form. Can we guarantee that we give ourselves or our pupils the opportunities for developing this wider range of skills? Given a choice in a text which can be read both verbally and visually (most current advertisements have both elements) what is our preferred modality?

It is at the level of values that the major challenges arise. The French can apparently tolerate a serious work in the format of a comic – can we? Is there a widely accepted list of films which we really ought to have seen to be counted as educated, in the same way as the work of particular novelists or poets is thought of as a standard part of our cultural background? Although the National Curriculum proposals (DES, 1989) do acknowledge the wider sense of text, how do they diverge from the received concept (there is no mention of 'writing' text other than verbal)?

If we can persuade ourselves that there is a point to thinking in broader terms about reading and communication, that we have some, and can improve, our credentials as media readers, that there are not only alternatives *within* traditional literacy but also alternatives *to* traditional literacy, we may find that the games perspective is one of the most useful means of developing the knowledge of and sensitivity to language that Kingman (1988) talks of. To learn what games are being played, what games there are to play, how to play them better is perhaps the best way to make sense of language as not simply a tool but a living experience of genuine interest and excitement.

References

Bellack, A. A. et al (1966) *The language of the classroom.* New York: Teachers College Press.
Berne, E. (1964) *The games people play.* London: André Deutsch.

Bloom, B. S. et al (1956) *Taxonomy of educational objectives, Book 1*. Cambridge, Mass.: M.I.T. Press.

Braddock, R. (1958) An extension to the 'Lasswell Formula'. *J. of Communication*, 8.

Davies, I. K. (1976) *Objectives in curriculum design*. Maidenhead: McGraw Hill.

DES (1984) *English from 5 to 16*. London: HMSO.

—— (1986) *English from 5 to 16* (2nd ed). London: HMSO.

Edwards, D. & Mercer, N. (1987) *Common knowledge*. London: Methuen.

Fiske, J. & Hartley, J. (1982) *Reading television*. London: Methuen.

Gillham, B. (1983) Values and the language curriculum. In Gillham, B. (ed) *Reading through the curriculum*. London: Heinemann.

Izod, J. (1984) *Reading the screen*. Harlow: Longman.

Kingman Committee (1988) *Report into the teaching of English language*. London: HMSO.

Lasswell, H. D. (1948) The structure and function of communication in society. In Bryson, L. (ed) *The communication of ideas*. New York: Harper.

McLuhan, M. (1964) *Understanding media*. London: Routledge Kegan Paul.

Shannon, C. & Weaver, W. (1949) *The mathematical theory of communication*. Urbana: Illinois University Press.

Sinclair, J. M. & Coulthard, R. M. (1975) *Towards an analysis of discourse*. London: Oxford University Press.

Wittgenstein, L. (1953) *Philosophical investigations*. Oxford: Blackwell.

Wray, D. (1989) Reading – the new debate. *Reading*, 23(1)

3 New developments in media education

Cary Bazalgette

Start by trying out a self-assessment task. Look at any audio-visual 'text' (a TV programme, a film) and think about whether you could, given time, 'make well-informed spoken or written responses to it, taking sophisticated account of matters such as dramatic, poetic or fictional structure, complexities of plot, development of character or theme, and the use of poetic and stylistic devices' and whether you could compare it with other works.

I am sure you will have no trouble making a sophisticated, knowledgeable reading of the particular text you chose, and will be able to articulate your responses if asked. In other words, you are able to demonstrate that you have reached attainment level 10 under the Reading profile component of the National Curriculum for English, as proposed by the Cox Committee – or you would have, if it weren't for one small point, which is that you are not expected to demonstrate those attainments in relation to a media text. All the skills and understandings you have exercised only 'count' in relation to literature.

That would be reasonable in a sense if it were being said that literature is the province of English and the media are not. But of course that isn't what the Cox Committee says. It says that you *are* expected to study media texts as part of English – indeed, as part of Reading – but the problem here is that, although you may be expected to study media texts within English, you are not expected to have the same sort of response to them as you are to literature. What you are supposed to be looking at in a media text is its intent to persuade or inform you. So you might be able to examine the text you chose in terms of the information it gives you, of its use of stereotyping, or the arguments it makes. But you wouldn't be able to investigate its use of narrative or character, its stylistic and generic features, the ways in which it pleased, moved or troubled you, and how these things were achieved.

There is another set of problems here too. In relation to a great many audio-visual texts (for example, *Neighbours* or *Star Wars*), it is hard to imagine a ten- or eleven-year-old who couldn't understand and respond to its narrative, generic and stylistic features, and who couldn't compare it to other texts. But, as far as the Cox Committee is concerned, the consideration of media texts only comes into the curriculum at the top of the junior school, and then only in terms of beginning to distinguish – in discussion – between fact and opinion. The uncomfortable probability, that children of eleven can achieve in relation to media texts what they are not expected to achieve in relation to literature before they are 16, is something the Cox Committee cannot – or will not – confront.

My intention here is not to snipe at Cox, however much it may seem so. Cox merely exemplifies the confusion at the interface between English and media education.

I want to present the arguments that have been made over the past few years for and against the recognition that the way that we engage with any media text – film, TV, radio, book – in some sense can and, indeed, ought to be seen as 'reading'. For now, I will use two catch-all terms, 'print literacy' and 'audio-visual literacy', rather than 'media literacy' or 'media education' and I will explain why later. I will then describe a particular way of thinking about how we should teach about the media, contextualized in terms of the work we've been doing over the last few years in BFI Education. And I will conclude with a question for literacy teachers.

The arguments against bringing print literacy and audio-visual literacy closer together are based on the simple empirical observation that everyone can watch TV but not everyone can read a book. That is to say, reading print is a complex process that has to be taught, whereas, it is alleged, everyone is naturally able to make sense of TV programmes, or photographs, or other audio-visual texts. What follows from that, apparently, on the premise that what is hard is good for you and what is easy isn't, is that reading is a worthwhile experience and watching TV is not. On the basis of this logic, it becomes possible to say that being 'lost in a book' is an admirable state to be in, while being lost in a TV programme lays you open to accusations of slack-jawed passivity, especially if you are a child. You are seen as uncritically swallowing what the screen pumps out – ingestion metaphors always seem to flourish in this scenario.

But it is worth recalling that new media have always given rise to the same kinds of anxiety. It was assumed about industrialised printing, as well as about cinema, and about radio, that they were irresponsibly making meanings available to vulnerable groups like women, servants or children who, it went without saying, were ill-equipped to deal with them. Such groups would be particularly prone to being 'taken in'; to being unable to distinguish between truth and falsehood, fact and opinion, in the new texts they were so naively enjoying.

So, having that history in mind, perhaps we can examine a little more dispassionately the differences and similarities between the ways in which we learn to process different kinds of text. Two observations are perhaps worth making here. One is that if children were 'bathed' in reading to the extent that they are bathed in TV watching – and I don't think even the most relentlessly literary household could ever equal the number of hours children spend, with friends, siblings and parents, learning how TV is watched – then who is to say that most children wouldn't come to school with basic reading skills already acquired and we would be saying that children 'naturally' learn to read in the home environment?

And the second observation is that making sense of TV – and radio, or cinema – *is* a learned skill. It is something young children can't do very well and it is something they get better at, and go on getting better at, broadening the range of what they can tackle throughout childhood. We are a bit short on good research on children's developmental understanding of TV. Most audience research funding has got diverted into market research or investigating the effects of sex and violence. But even so, most infant teachers know that four- and five-year-olds often cannot hold in their heads or even follow the narrative of a lot of the TV or films they watch. This isn't only because the content may be too sophisticated but because they are just not following the grammar of the framing and editing; for example, they might perceive a cut to a close-up as being a cut to a different, larger object.

However, these observations do not necessarily dispose of the arguments against bringing print literacy and audio-visual literacy closer together. The ground then shifts to acknowledging that audio-visual literacy is learned, but suggesting that children learn it easily, by themselves, and therefore schools need not concern themselves with it. In fact some inflections of this argument say that the very ease of acquiring audio-visual literacy makes problems for, or even interferes with, the acquisition of print literacy. Although these arguments are now increasingly being abandoned, they still inflect the ways in which people's thinking moves towards the notion that the role of audio-visual media in people's lives has to be confronted in the context of ideas about literacy. But this isn't a simple shift from one position to another. For a start, it depends, of course, on what you mean by literacy. This is not the context in which to go into all the different inflections of that term. Suffice it to say that when it gets used in the audio-visual context, it gets inflected again by the different ways in which people define the nature and function of audio-visual media. So the term 'literacy' when applied to audio-visual media tends to get used in confusingly different ways and perhaps these need clarification.

Broadly speaking, there are three ways in which arguments for a link between print literacy and audio-visual literacy tend to be made.

Argument 1: A-V literacy is a useful aid to learning

This is the 'conservative' view: one in which it goes without saying that print is the most important medium. It is premised on the assumption that the audio-visual media are just neutral channels and are interesting for teachers only in terms of the uses to which they can be put. For example, pictures help to clarify the meaning of texts; taped versions of stories motivate children to take an interest in literature; the graphics that surround us in everyday life, and the variety of language uses in the media, help with children's understanding of print and of language; audio-visual teaching materials can be an efficient way of putting across information.

Argument 2: A-V literacy should be integrated with print literacy

This is the 'radical' argument which is based on the premise that audio-visual media and print media are effectively the same. It can thus be said that we 'read' and 'write' media 'texts'; that the audio-visual competences that children bring to school with them should be recognised and valued and that by doing this we may well enhance and accelerate children's acquisition of print literacy; that true literacy is in fact media literacy.

Argument 3: 'Literacy' needs rethinking

This is essentially a more cautious version of argument (2). It sees argument (2) as pragmatic: a necessary strategy at the moment in order to get educators to acknowledge the importance of the visual, but at the same time acknowledges the differences between audio-visual and print media and argues for more research into the links between them and into how audio-visual competences are acquired.

I should now explain why I have not used the term 'media education' so far. There is a simple basic reason: if 'the media' means all the ways in which meanings can be communicated to numbers of people, then print is also a medium. So, anything that calls itself media education cannot logically avoid addressing all media, from books to satellite TV. Given that assertion, you will see that media education – at least as I am describing it – is based on either or both of arguments (2) and (3), but not on argument (1), which seeks to make a distinction between audio-visual media and print media, seeing the former as useful only in the service of the latter.

It is likely that you will, or may already have, come across accounts of media education that share aspects of all three arguments or are even just based on the first argument. The Cox proposals are a good example of the kind of confusion I mean. Nevertheless, I shall argue that the best and most productive and interesting forms of media education are those that are based on at least some of the second and third arguments.

Some historical context may be helpful here. Throughout the 1980s there has been a shift away from thinking that teaching about the media was best taken care of in specialist courses such as media studies, communication studies or film studies, taking place mainly on an optional basis in the upper secondary school and above. The thinking moved towards the idea that there should *also* (not 'instead') be a general provision for media education throughout compulsory schooling. Two things gave a particular impetus to this kind of thinking. One was the DES report, *Popular TV and schoolchildren*, which came out in 1983 and, amongst other things, proposed that 'specialist courses in media studies are not enough: all teachers should be involved in examining and discussing television programmes with young people'. It also proposed the setting up of regional working groups in England to follow up the report's proposals. These all inevitably included people committed to the broader remit of media education, and also had the useful function of bringing together media educators and broadcasters, who had previously tended to regard one another with suspicion.

The other impetus was of course the initiation of the National Curriculum, with the first discussion document in July 1987. Media teachers had to decide how best to respond to a document that appeared to carve up the curriculum in terms of timetable allocations and of course made no mention of media education whatsoever. Although there was understandably a clamour of anguish from specialist media teachers in secondary schools and colleges who saw their first priority as fighting for media studies in 'the ten per cent' non-foundation subject time, there were also significant numbers of people who saw this as the opportunity to suggest that a modern curriculum could not afford to ignore the media, and a way had to be found of including media education in the core curriculum. What eventually happened was that 'media studies' [sic] was designated a cross-curricular theme but was also given to the English Working Group for specific consideration within English. (It is interesting, incidentally, that their remit asked them to consider how media studies could be taught through English, but Cox has tended to turn this around and show how media studies can be of service to English – ie back to argument (1).)

While all this was going on, increasing numbers of primary and lower secondary teachers were already developing ways of teaching about the media with younger age-groups. We brought a number of these people together at the BFI in 1985 to discuss their work and how we could support it, and out of that group we formed a working party that later gave itself the grandiose title BFI/DES National Working Party for Primary Media Education and set itself the task of looking at what good practice in primary media education might look like. It is worth remembering that not long before this it was commonplace to hear it said that learning about the media would be far too hard for junior school children to undertake, let alone infants, with the not entirely spurious justification that media studies courses dealt with tough theoretical concepts derived from courses in higher education. So our working party really had to start from basics, on the assumption that we weren't going to dilute the 'easy bits' of the theories even more, but were going to look at the media knowledge children brought to school and how that could and should be developed over a six year period. We also wanted to look at how such work could be integrated into the primary curriculum, not just tacked on as yet another extra.

We worked on this for three years and I won't go through all the problems and dead ends and confusions we got ourselves into. Suffice it to say that, after about 18 months, we became aware that it just did not work to try and describe media education in terms of sets of practices – things children might do in the classroom – or in terms of skills, or in terms of media forms or technologies (eg children ought to know about television and cinema and radio and . . . do we include the music industry? . . . what about computers? etc). We had to identify the *conceptual* elements of media education – what we thought children ought to know about and understand. From that framework, the skills and the study objects and the classroom practice would follow, though obviously our discussion of the conceptual framework was based on our experience of classroom practice and on our understandings about where children were starting from, ie the media knowledge they brought to school with them.

After a good deal of debate we identified six areas that we thought were basic enough for even the youngest children to get a purchase on them, but at the same time were capable of being developed to sophisticated levels. These areas are outlined in the following chart (Figure 3.1), which shows how each area can be signalled by a simple question, versions of which can be made accessible to very young children. The chart appears in *Primary media education: a curriculum statement* (BFI, 1989). It is interesting that Cox only identifies *one* conceptual area – language – although there is clearly a conceptual framework not dissimilar to ours lurking within the proposals. Audience, authorship, genre and narrative are there; what is missing is the wider sense of 'institutions' that for us underlies the concepts of both audience and authorship: how, and why, texts get produced and circulated. Also missing is the concept of 'representation' which for us is a crucial underpinning of any understanding of 'stereotype', 'realism' or 'bias'. Children need to explore the *range* of ways in which

Figure 3.1 SIGNPOST QUESTIONS

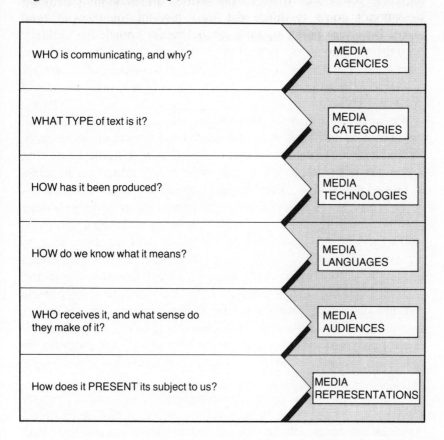

texts may legitimately relate to the real world, before they can deal productively with such terms.

You will notice that there is nothing about this conceptual structure that necessarily links it only to the study of audio-visual texts. To argue, as Cox seems to do, that questions about institutions or representation are only relevant to media texts is to imply that only audio-visual media are ideologically suspect and literature is always innocent. But I would argue that the questions this structure makes possible are the ones we need in order to extend the possible meanings of any text, and to extend the range of texts available to us. This means, extending our pleasures as well as our understandings.

For media teachers, arguments that seek to describe audio-visual competence as 'literacy' are exciting and thought-provoking as well as a useful strategy. But my concluding question is, how are they regarded by literacy teachers?

4 Context, continuity and communication in learning

Neil Mercer

The theme 'Communication and learning' is open to a variety of interpretations. There are articles on learning *about* communication, covering areas like 'language awareness' and 'media education'. There are many which are about learning *to* communicate – the development of literacy, helping children make good use of the new technology, and so on. There are also some which, like mine, are about communication *in* learning, or the examination of teaching and learning as a communicative process. It is not my intention here to present detailed information about any one particular research project. What I present instead is a personal view of the relationship between communication and learning, and a case for why that relationship is worthy of close attention by researchers and teachers.

My opinion is that education would benefit considerably if it was more widely accepted that communication and learning are almost inextricably bound up together. Now it may seem that it is quite commonsensically true that education is a communicative process, and that one would have to look very hard for even a straw man to argue about the idea that we learn through communication. But common sense also justifies those critics of our primary schools who say that children spend too much time 'just talking' when they should be learning. It tells us that children succeed or fail in schools because of their individual attributes, their IQs not their communicative experiences. Common sense also tells us that work entails action, not talk, and that learning is something best achieved in solitude, when one is *incommunicado*. The problem with common sense is that it can be invoked to support almost anything you want it to. We have to penetrate common sense explanations if we want to discover anything worth knowing about education.

If we accept that education is social and communicative, we might then consider three questions:

1   Why is so much of education still conducted as though it isn't, as though it's really to do with individuals thinking and learning and acting in isolation?
2   What does a 'social and communicative', as opposed to an 'individualistic', perspective on learning actually mean?
3   What can a truly communicative perspective on learning contribute to educational practice?

The first issue is not so hard to address. Many people with a strong influence on education have said, in so many words, that the development of knowledge and intelligence is a matter of individual activity, adaptation, cognition. Burt, Skinner and Piaget offered contrasting images of the learner, but always the individual learner. Of these three, Piaget's has undoubtedly been the strongest influence on modern British education. For him, the essence of cognitive development is the adaptation of a lone organism to its environment (Piaget, 1969: see also Bruner, 1985). Action, not communication, is the key to learning.

The Plowden Report (1967), which reflected Piaget's views, did little to encourage a communicative ideology in British teaching. Although it made some positive references to group activity, it stated clearly that 'verbal explanation, in advance of understanding based on experience, may be an obstacle to learning, and children's knowledge of the right words may conceal from teachers their lack of understanding' (para. 535). In its 'child-centred' classroom, talking and reading were given much less importance as tools of learning, especially in mathematics and science, than 'hands on' activity and individual discoveries.

The teaching of reading is one area of education practice less evidently influenced by Piagetian theory. But as UK Reading Association members are particularly aware, most reading research has focused on how individuals process print; and most material for teaching reading has been designed with the prime aim of helping individuals to learn to recognise letters and words rather than to teach children or adults how to begin using a written form of communication.

Communicative perspectives

There are now some lines of educational research which are not dominated by individualistic perspectives. Those which I find most illuminating share the following features:

- they deal with a process of 'teaching-and-learning', and not just 'learning' as an individualised activity;
- they analyse the content of communication, and not just its form or structure;
- they assert that all communication is context-dependent (and so deal with context as well as content).

I will offer here two distinct illustrative examples of such kinds of research.

1 Anthropological research which treats literacy as social practice.
2 Socio-cognitive research on classroom communication.

I will discuss the first briefly, and then go on to use the second example (which represents the research I know best) to elaborate on the concepts of *continuity* and *context*.

Literacy as social practice

This line of research is well represented by that of Street (1984), Scribner & Cole (1981) and Heath (1983). One of its messages is that there isn't just one thing called 'literacy', there are lots of 'literacies' and which ones you acquire will depend on who you are and where you grow up. Literacy is not depicted as a set of abstract skills, but as social practice, a cultural phenomenon. The literacy practices people use in any particular set of social circumstances will reflect the sense they make of those circumstances, the way they contextualize the literacy event.

For instance, Heath (1982, 1983) takes the notion of 'stories' and shows that, because of the different cultures of the black and white working class communities in which they grow up, North American children living just a few miles apart have almost irreconcilable ideas about what a story is. For the children of the black community Heath called 'Trackton', stories are oral fantasies, improvisations based loosely on experience which can be modified whenever they are performed to real audiences. For the white working class children of 'Roadville', stories are accounts you are told, or which you read (typically in the Bible). They are truths, god-given sometimes, and if you change them you get them wrong. So Heath is able to come up with the memorable statement that ...

'... for Roadville, Trackton's stories would be lies: for Trackton, Roadville's stories would not even count as stories.' (Heath, 1983, p 189)

Crucially, both these conceptions of a story are different from the idea of story which Trackton and Roadville's children encounter in school. What school literacy does in that part of the world is bring three different communicative practices into conflict – a conflict which, as Heath relates, is rarely successfully resolved.

Classroom communication

An interesting and important aspect of the conflict between communicative practices which Heath describes is that it is never normally brought out into the open and discussed in classrooms. Such things rarely are, at home or abroad. Yet a key element of the communicative process of education must be the development of an understanding which is shared. Teachers and learners need to have shared – or at least compatible – views of what they think they are doing and why they are doing it. Contrary to Plowden's assertion, 'verbal explanation' can make something that seems like a perfectly pointless exercise into a quite meaningful one. When some of the teachers in Heath's study did develop a shared sense of purpose with the children, a new kind of progress was made. Think back on your own educational experience. If I'd been told in the 'O' level maths class what 'integration' and 'differentiation' were *for*, I might have remembered how to do them! One of the ways that adult literacy tuition sometimes succeeds when school has previously failed, is by basing instruction on the real life literacy demands of people's lives, such as in occupational training. The purpose, the reason for becoming literate, is clear to both teacher and learner, and literacy is contextualized by other, non-literary social practices.

Context

My own research, with Derek Edwards and Janet Maybin, has looked at communications between those involved in teaching and learning, in schools and in adult education (eg Edwards & Mercer, 1987; Mercer & Edwards, 1987; Mercer, Edwards & Maybin, 1988). For theory, we have looked to Vygotsky (eg 1966, 1978) and Bruner (eg 1986), not Piaget. We have tried to describe how knowledge is jointly constructed, and the ways in which that constructive process succeeds and fails. We also want to know what sense participants make of what they do, and the extent to which that understanding or interpretation is mutual.

To do this, we have analysed the discourse of classrooms, looked at what has been done and written in educational activities and talked to teachers and learners about what they have done. Unlike more linguistics-based discourse analysts (eg Stubbs, 1981; Sinclair & Coulthard, 1975), we are primarily interested in the content and function of talk rather than its form or structure: we analyse talk to see what people talk about, and not to identify linguistic units or cohesive structures. And it is our interest in *content* which generated our particular concern with *context*.

By the 'context' of a conversation I mean everything that the participants know and understand (over and above that which is explicit in what they say) which they use to make sense of what is said and done. 'Context' doesn't mean those features of the physical environment which co-exist with the discourse, or the speakers' gestures and other non-verbal communications which accompany it. Those things are, of course, part of what the context may be *constructed from*. Speakers may invoke physical objects and events; but if they don't, these things are not really part of the context. Likewise for writers. Examine the quality of the paper on which these words are written. That paper was not part of the context of our communication as writer and audience. Now I have invoked it, and so it is.

'Context' is then a mental, not a physical, phenomenon. It is the luggage, the caravan of shared rememberings which conversationalists carry with them because it is needed to sustain their talk.

To add to the mix of metaphors, it is the invisible two-thirds of the iceberg which keeps the visible part, the talk, afloat.

An old-fashioned model of communication, which can still be found in some communication studies textbooks, is of a process whereby a message goes from a transmitter to a receiver. Of course, communication requires not only the receipt of a message, but for that message to be intelligible to the receiver. And the intelligibility of any message depends on the existence of a contextual frame of reference, shared by the communicating parties, which will support the message. Any satisfactory model of communication must incorporate the process of building this shared frame of reference. And this applies just as much to communication through the print media, television and new electronic methods of communicating like 'e-mail' as it does to face-to-face conversation.

Continuity

Context is the basis of continuity in learning. Good teachers contextualize new experiences for children by relating them to past experiences. They 'scaffold' learning (Bruner, 1985) through communication and interaction. New understandings may then be built on the secure foundations of existing knowledge, or allow the revision of what was hitherto known and understood.

We should be able to admit that one important function of education is as a system for assisting the creation and continuity of culture, without feeling that this is letting traditional education at its worst in through the back door. We can recognise culture and continuity without returning to Mr Gradgrind and his pitchers full of facts or a neo-Victorian ethnocentric curriculum. We needn't lose the insights into active learning and creativity which child-centred education has given us. But contrary to the most extreme versions of progressive education, children don't necessarily have to discover things to understand them. They don't need to reinvent the wheel, Newton's laws, Jane Austen's novels or LOGO because there is someone else who knows about these things and can share them. The important thing is that in the sharing, through the communication, the knowledge and understanding come to belong to the children. In Bruner's (1983) terms, there must be 'handover', so that the learners come to possess what they have learnt. Readers do need to discover what

Jane Austen means to them. It is in dealing with the role of communication and culture in learning that the theories of Vygotsky (1966, 1978; see also Wertsch, 1985) are more useful than those of Piaget.

Educational implications

I will now return to the last of the three considerations I set out at the beginning of this paper: what can a communicative perspective on learning contribute to the practice of education? What are the implications of the kind of research I have been describing for how education is defined and carried out? I feel I can deal with this best by reference to four particular educational topics which interest me, and to which I have found it useful to apply a communicative perspective.

1 Defining the role of the teacher

One problem with the progressive, Piagetian-influenced model of learning is that it denies the teacher an active, participative role in the learning process. The traditional, didactic model of education, on the other hand, ignores the need for learners to actively participate in the construction of knowledge and understanding. A communicative perspective emphasises that teachers and learners must successfully build a contextual framework of knowledge and understanding if education is to be achieved. The role of a teacher seen from this perspective is an active one. In Bruner's terms, it is someone who 'scaffolds' the experience of a learner, and does not just provide 'learning environments'. A communicative perspective also encourages teachers to share the purposes, the point, of educational activities with learners. For teachers, then, the stark, crude choice between the didactic, authoritarian pedagogy of traditional education and the discovery-led, 'invisible' pedagogy of high progressivism is circumvented. Instead there emerges a conception of a good teacher as one who can make the right judgements about when to tell, when to ask, when to instruct, and when to stand well clear and only facilitate. A communicative approach to learning can provide teachers with a rationale for making these difficult judgements.

2   Reading and learning

All of us here probably accept that a model of reading which has a lone reader grappling with a text, decoding that text through rules of phonics, grammar and so on is an inadequate model, psychologically, because it doesn't represent the way that people really read. But the 'lone reader' model is something that still needs to be rejected as a figment of educational ideology, because it ignores the ways that reading matter is, or can be, used to best advantage in education. The things that students read in school – Shakespeare, science textbooks, worksheets or whatever – are familiar too to their teachers. Such texts are an important source of potential material for building up a common knowledge, a universe of discourse, a foundation for sharing and developing continuity in educational thought. Reading is thus part of the interactive process of teaching and learning, and can be organised accordingly.

3   Collaborative learning

Although some teachers have long recognised the value of children collaborating and communicating together while they learn, collaborative learning has only recently begun to achieve legitimacy as a pedagogic technique within the dominant educational ideology. The continuing influence of those individualistic psychologies referred to earlier has certainly helped to keep it out in the cold. And some of the most insightful research on collaboration and learning (eg Barnes & Todd, 1977) lacked a strong theoretical base. The 'neo-Piagetians' have valiantly tried to accommodate collaboration within their theoretical framework (see eg Mugny, Perret-Clermont & Doise, 1981), but this has always seemed to me at best a 'grafting-on' exercise. Now, with the emergence of a more genuinely social, communicative cognitive perspective derived from Vygotsky rather than Piaget, more interesting and rewarding research on collaborative problem solving by children (see eg Light & Perret-Clermont, 1989; Rogoff, 1989) and adults (eg Edwards & Middleton, 1986) is emerging. And in educational practice, the current activities of the National Oracy Project (as reported in their regular newsletter *Talk*) show that many teachers are using the new legitimacy which the project has given to classroom talk to develop collaborative pedagogies.

In the past, justifications for the use of any collaborative activities in the classroom tended to be of the 'social skills' or 'personal and social development' kind: they help children to co-operate, and that in itself is good. But now developments in research and practice should encourage the use of such activities for cognitive, curriculum-related reasons, as it is realised more how important discourse can be for converting mere experience into knowledge, something shared and understood; and how young children can achieve new levels of understanding with the help of their friends (Bruner, 1985).

4 Assessment

A communicative perspective draws attention to whether teachers and learners have the same understanding of the purpose and nature of educational activities. This is particularly relevant to *assessment*. It is surprising how little attention has been given to the issue of whether teachers and learners, the assessor and the person being assessed, have a shared understanding of the criteria for success, against which performances will be evaluated. As Janet Maybin (1988), amongst others, has argued, such matters are given too little attention by those responsible for the design and administration of new assessment instruments. And in the classroom it is only rarely that such things are discussed, brought out in the open, made explicit. When anyone asks children what they think is the point and purpose of what they are expected to do in school, the answers are often very revealing.

My colleagues and I have discussed these kinds of things in more detail elsewhere (eg Edwards & Mercer, 1987; Mercer, Edwards & Maybin, 1988). Here, I simply offer a couple of relevant anecdotes.

One East Anglian teacher told me how she had asked some twelve-year-olds what they thought about doing poetry in school, what they liked and didn't like. Quite a few said they didn't like it. When asked why, one said 'Well, it's all right when you have to read poems and talk about it; but then we always have to *solve* them.' Many of the children thought there was a 'right answer' to the poem, which they had to find to succeed.

I talked to some other secondary children who had been doing oracy assessment tasks – the sorts of exercises which may well emerge as Standard Assessment Tasks for talking and listening under the National Curriculum – and they had some very diverse ideas about what they were being assessed on. Some thought that a 'good performance' was one in which they made no mistakes, no slips of the tongue, hesitations etc (rather like in the radio programme 'Just a minute'); others thought it was entirely the knowledge content of what they said that counted. These two views could obviously lead to quite different attempts at a good performance.

This is no ivory tower, academic research problem. On the eve of the National Curriculum, I am sure that many of us here find much to agree with in the latest proposals for *English for ages 5–16* (DES, 1989). But there are good reasons for thinking that teaching and learning under the National Curriculum is going to be assessment-led. We don't really know yet what that assessment will be like, and it could push a lot of good intentions and principles expressed in the curriculum documentation we have seen so far into the background. The proposals for *English 5–16* recognise assessment problems, but they don't provide the solutions. For example, in discussing the assessment of reading, they say

'. . . many existing tests [being used in primary schools] use decontextualized approaches which do not adequately assess children's understanding of meaning.' (DES, 1989, para. 16.49)

In relation to writing they also argue against the use of 'decontextualized tests or exercises' (para. 17.63), and point out the need for schools to formulate guidelines on assessment which can:

'clarify aims and objectives in setting, and responding to, written work, for the benefit of pupils, staff and parents. Pupils, especially, might increase their understanding of how they learn.' (para. 17.71)

This is good advice. We can only hope that the assessment procedures which are adopted under the National Curriculum reflect it, and recognise that assessment, like the rest of education, is a communicative, contextualized process. Then perhaps we can begin to believe that the cold war between 'traditional' and 'progressive' pedagogies is over and we have entered an era of 'communicative' education.

References

Barnes, D. & Todd, F. (1977) *Communication and learning in small groups.* London: Routledge & Kegan Paul.

Bruner, J. S. (1983) *Child's talk.* London: Oxford University Press.

—— (1985) 'Vygotsky: a historical and conceptual perspective.' In Wertsch, J. V. (ed) *Culture, communication and cognition: Vygotskian perspectives.* Cambridge: Cambridge University Press.

—— (1986) *Actual minds, possible worlds.* London: Harvard University Press.

DES (1989) *English for ages 5 to 16: proposals of the Secretary of State for Education and Science and the Secretary of State for Wales.* London: HMSO.

Edwards, D. & Mercer, N. (1987) *Common knowledge: the development of understanding in the classroom.* London: Routledge.

Edwards, D. & Middleton, D. (1986) Joint remembering: constructing an account of shared experience. *Discourse Processes*, 9, pp 423–59.

Heath, S. B. (1982) What no bedtime story means: narrative skills at home and school. *Language and Society*, 11, pp 49–76.

—— (1983) *Ways with words.* Cambridge: Cambridge University Press.

Light, P. & Perret-Clermont, A. N. (1989) Social context effects in learning and testing. In Gellatly, A., Rogers, D. & Sloboda, J. (eds) *Cognition and social worlds.* Oxford: Oxford University Press.

Maybin, J. (1988) A critical review of the DES Assessment of Performance Unit's Oracy Survey. *English in Education*, 22, 1, pp 3–18.

Mercer, N. & Edwards, D. (1987) The development of understanding in a group of adults working together. *Open Learning*, 2, 2, pp 22–28.

Mercer, N., Edwards, D. & Maybin, J. (1988) Putting context into oracy: the construction of shared knowledge through classroom discourse. In Maclure, M., Phillips, T. & Wilkinson, A. (eds) *Oracy matters.* Milton Keynes: Open University Press.

Mugny, G., Perret-Clermont, A. N. & Doise , W. (1981) Interpersonal co-ordinations and sociological differences in the construction of the intellect. In Stephenson, G. and Davis, J. (eds) *Progress in applied social psychology, vol 1.* Chichester: Wiley.

Piaget, J. (1969) A genetic approach to the psychology of thought. In de Cecco, J. (ed) *The Psychology of language, thought and instruction.* London: Holt, Reinhart & Winston.

Plowden Report (1967) *Children and their primary schools.* London: Central Advisory Council for Education.

Rogoff, B. (1989) The joint socialization of development by young children and adults. In Gellatly, A., Rogers, D. & Sloboda, J. (eds) *Cognition and social worlds.* Oxford: Oxford University Press.

Scribner, S. & Cole, M. (1981) *The Psychology of literacy.* London: Harvard University Press.

Sinclair, J. McH. & Coulthard, M. (1975) *Towards an analysis of discourse.* London: Oxford University Press.

Street, B. V. (1984) *Literacy in theory and practice.* Cambridge: Cambridge University Press.

Stubbs, M. (1981) Scratching the surface: linguistic data in educational research. In Adelman, C. (ed) *Uttering, muttering: collecting, using and reporting talk for social and educational research.* London: Grant McIntyre.

Vygotsky, L. S. (1966) Development of the higher mental functions. In Leontièv, A., Luria, A. & Smirnov, A. (eds) *Psychological research in the USSR, vol 1.* Moscow: Progress Publishing.

—— (1978) *Mind in society: the development of higher psychological processes.* London: Harvard University Press.

Wertsch, J. V. (ed) *Culture, communication and cognition: Vygotskian perspectives.* Cambridge: Cambridge University Press.

5 Representations of literacy in the media

Peter Putnis

On the face of it one wouldn't expect literacy to be a particularly newsworthy subject. How often would potential items concerning literacy meet such criteria of newsworthiness as 'conflict', 'the extreme and unusual' or 'involving celebrities and political figures'? One might expect the occasional 'human interest' story but, beyond that, literacy does not seem to be the stuff of news.

Yet literacy does make news. Why is this so, and what does it mean for the way in which the public at large perceive literacy issues? Furthermore, what are the implications of the way literacy is constructed in the media for those of us who have a professional interest in literacy? These are amongst the questions which will be discussed in this chapter.

What is the literacy debate really all about? On one level it is what it seems – a debate about how well people can read and write, about how many people can't and why they can't, and about how well the education system performs in this respect. But this is by no means *all* that the literacy debate is about. It also concerns *what* is read, particularly by young people, and how it might affect them. And it concerns *how* people write – the particular linguistic forms they use – and about inferences that are drawn from these usages about attitudes and personality traits, desirable or undesirable. Further, the debate invokes and mobilises larger personal and social issues: social progress or decline; discipline versus permissiveness; social order versus anarchy; nostalgia for the mythic golden age of one's youth coupled with fear of an apocalyptic future. In short, the literacy debate is a site upon which a myriad of personal and societal anxieties, prejudices and ideologies materialise and contest. Professionals dealing with the public must take cognisance of these wider associations of literacy.

This chapter presents an Australian case study of the representation of literacy in the media. It analyses the popular discourse or literacy via an examination of all stories in Brisbane's major daily newspaper, *The Courier-Mail*, published over the four year period 1984–1987 which use the word 'literacy'. The aim is to understand better how people conceive of and talk about literacy in order to help account for the ubiquity and cultural and political force of the literacy debate. The paper will highlight the character-istic ways in which the issue of literacy is constructed as a 'prob-lem', and the ways in which the media both reflect and propagate certain typical representations of the issue. The patterns of repre-sentation it describes will be recognised as having relevance to the situation in the United Kingdom. But before moving on to the detailed analysis, some preliminary points need to be made.

What is literacy?

Attempts to define and codify standards of literacy in schools go back at least to the nineteenth century. As Little (1978, p 3) notes, the OED dates the notion of 'educational standards' from 1876 when in England the Revised Code for Testing Standards I–VI in elementary schools was established. But despite unceasing attempts at definition literacy remains an elusive concept – inevit-ably so, given that the term acts as a 'coat-hanger' for competence in a great variety of cultural practices ranging from looking up a telephone book to reading Shakespeare, from signing one's name to writing an essay. Recently, of course, the term has been ex-tended in such phrases as 'computer literacy' and 'cultural liter-acy'. The very vagueness of the term makes it fertile ground for ideological work. As Johnson (1980, p 82) comments on the 'liter-acy problem':

'The problem looks simple because it is overtly only a question of educational standards; but the issue is also vague, difficult to pin down, and hence ideologically useful in the promotion of social unease and the need for authority.'

A matter of measurement?

The literacy debate comes to us in the guise of an empirical argument capable of empirical resolution. All the trappings are there – tests, standards, statistics, scores. The 'problem' is pre-

sented as measurable and controllable. The question is, has there
been a decline in standards or not? A study must be done to
resolve the matter once and for all! Why is it that despite extensive
empirical studies which demonstrate that there has not been a
decline (Little, 1985) the matter is not resolved, at least as far as
the popular debate is concerned? The empirical studies, far from
resolving the issue, merely become further chips in what is a
deeper game. For example Parkin (1984) has described the sensa-
tional reporting of the 1976 Australian Council for Educational
Research study into literacy and numeracy in Australian Schools
(Keeves & Bourke, 1976). The study itself, with its complex
statistical tables, was cautious in its findings, yet was reported by
the media within the 'crisis/decline' formula. According to Peter
Samuel in *The Bulletin*, the study showed an 'alarming failure of
education.' The headline was 'Australia's Education Scandal:
We're turning out millions of dunces' (Samuel, 1976). This set the
tone for further media debate on the Report. The seemingly
objective evidence of the study was mobilised to legitimate an
attack on State schools.

The language of the gods

Attitudes within a community towards various forms of a language
reflect the power structure of that community. Most societies have
one particular language form which is regarded as the 'best' or
'purest'. This is sometimes the language of priests (hence closer to
the divine originator), sometimes of the metropolis and sometimes, as in the English tradition, the language of the upper-
classes, in this case given added legitimacy by being associated
with royalty – hence the King's or Queen's English. This form is
also generally associated with some golden age before a linguistic
fall. Few can measure up to the ideal. Furthermore, extralinguis-
tic judgements are made about people according to their language
use. Surface features of language (often paradoxically referred to
as the 'basics') become conventional signs for status, intelligence
and even moral worth.

Literacy and ideology

Street (1984) contrasts two broad approaches to literacy: the
'autonomous' model and the 'ideological' model. The former

treats literacy as a 'neutral' technology. Teaching literacy is teaching a technical skill that the individual can go on to utilise as he or she wishes. Literacy also develops intellectual qualities, particularly abstract thinking, and in general enhances personal autonomy and efficacy. His 'ideological' model (broadly supported in this paper) recognises that teaching literacy is not just a matter of imparting technical skills. 'Literacy' is a set of social practices and relations. Learning literacy is learning particular roles, forms of interaction and ways of thinking. As Street puts it (1984, p 8), 'the meaning of literacy depends upon the social institutions in which it is embedded'.

Literacy in The Courier-Mail

Let me now turn to this case study of the representation of literacy in Brisbane's *The Courier-Mail*. In the four years 1984–1987 there were 151 newspaper items using the word 'literacy': 41 in 1984, 37 in 1985, 41 in 1986 and 32 in 1987. 123 of these refer to reading and writing skills. Most of the remainder are about computer literacy though there are also references to economic literacy, visual literacy and so forth. Of the 123 stories, 13 include only insignificant passing references to literacy. Of the remaining 110, six are overseas stories and 104 are domestic ones. There were two editorials and 15 letters, with the remainder news items and features.

In the following analysis the 110 stories in which literacy is a significant part of the content are examined with a view to highlighting characteristic ways in which literacy is perceived and prescribed.

When literacy (not illiteracy) is a threat

Two stories – one about Nicaragua, the other about Afghanistan – reverse our culture's commonsense perception of literacy being positive and illiteracy negative in a way that reveals the political dimensions of literacy. Literacy is a threat when it is promoted by one's ideological adversaries. It then becomes a tool of propaganda and it is better to leave the people illiterate. In Nicaragua 'the Sandinistas have doubled literacy to almost 90 per cent'. However 'the price being paid for this is that the children are being taught only Marxist propaganda' (27/11/84). In Afghanistan, the Russian claims that they intended to bring literacy to the people can be viewed in a similar way. As the main interviewee in the Afghanistan story puts it, 'Literacy is a western concept. Islam has a rich oral tradition. That is one of the reasons why the Soviet propaganda machine didn't work on these people. The Afghans would rather be illiterate than to be told what they had to read' (8/8/87).

The formulations in these stories – literacy as a means of social/ ideological control and illiteracy as a form of resistance – have little currency in the contemporary debate. However, they strongly echo an earlier stage of that debate when the political issues were more explicit.

In 1809 when Tom Paine died it has been estimated that the circulation of his *Rights of Man* had gone as high as one and a half million at a time when the total population of the British Isles was no more than sixteen million (Donald, 1983, p 36). For the authorities it was literacy that was the problem over which they eventually asserted control through the development of mass schooling. Through mass education literacy could be transformed from a threat to political stability to a new means of regulation and discipline, an avenue for character formation.

In Queensland around 1900, politicians and educationalists were quite explicit about the ideological role of schooling. While universal literacy was the avowed aim of State schooling, it is clear that this was to be restricted to 'necessary literacy', conceived in terms of citizenship and manpower requirements. J. G. Anderson, Queensland's Under-secretary for Public-Instruction, arguing against the need for any secondary schooling, warned of 'the dangers of an educated proletariat' (Anderson, 1897, p 981) and the creation of 'a class mentally disqualified to earn a living under the conditions of the time' (1897, p 981). In Queensland around 1900 the politically ambiguous status of education was well recognised. Too much was a threat, too little dysfunctional. Central to this issue was ensuring that appropriate forms of language and of interaction were taught – the 'Queen's English' in Queensland, one might say.

While the ideological role of literacy teaching is rarely as explicitly stated in the contemporary debate as in the earlier part of this century, revealing echoes of it can nevertheless be heard. Arguments ostensibly for greater attention to literacy are never too distinct from arguments for the formation of 'appropriate' attitudes. A report of the concerns of the Australian Chamber of

Commerce – 'businessmen express concern at the basic literacy skills of school leavers' – continues, 'the second and *related* issue is the attitude of youth' (my emphasis), and goes on to criticise the 'she'll be right' approach and attitudes to work and authority (12/11/85). Then there is the plan of the Queensland Confederation of Industry to launch its own 'State-wide industry entrance tests for school-leavers' because of the inadequacy of school testing. The exam would assess 'literacy skills and test a basic understanding of such things as productivity and unions'. The test would 'force schools to teach about industry' (18/6/87). In the political arena a conservative stance on literacy has become an integral part of a larger conservative agenda clustered around the slogan 'back to the basics' and is also used as a scapegoat for social problems, especially youth unemployment.

Literacy as a measure of development

In three stories the rate of literacy is used as a measure of development or lack of it in third world countries and in one as a measure of the progress of Australian Aboriginals. With respect to the third world, literacy becomes part of a statistical formula as in this description of Nepal: 'The pressures are enormous for a nation with a population of more than 15 million, an average life expectancy of 46, a per capita income of less than $200, and a literacy rate of 23 per cent' (1/7/85). The Australian story has the then Queensland Premier saying that 'Queensland's Aboriginals and Torres Strait Islanders were among the best treated indigenous people in the world' and that 'an example of progress was that literacy amongst Aboriginals and Islanders was now the norm' (30/1/84).

This use of an ethnocentric yardstick of literacy as an 'objective' measure of development (in the case of the Aboriginals, for development read assimilation) can reverberate back into discussions of literacy in white Australia. Stories of one million Australians being illiterate (18/12/84) threaten our self-concept as an 'advanced' country.

The romance of the word

The concern about literacy standards is sometimes presented as a pragmatic, utilitarian concern. The population needs to be 'functionally literate'. Yet there is a strong current of almost religious fervour in the debate, predicated on a view of English, or more correctly a particular variety of it, as almost sacred. It must be kept inviolate in the face of the forces of desecration.

A classic statement of this position in Australian educational history was in the Queensland Director of Education's 1905 Report. He describes English as a stately tree which, unfortunately, is 'exposed to every blast that blows, in town or country, the reek of the shop, the fume of the mine, the sulphurous passage of the bullock dray'. Given that in Queensland language is 'blasted, broken, twisted and torn' he concludes that 'most of the influences outside school are to a greater or less extent against the school in its work of teaching English' (Ewart, 1906, p 1335). The school-room becomes a cultural and moral oasis fortified against the everyday life and language of working-class Queenslanders. Literacy education is a contest between the 'Queen's English', with its moral high-ground, and Queensland English (the forms actually spoken by the people) which signals a fallen state.

In the contemporary debate we find echoes of this mythology. Three stories engage it directly, while in many others it functions as an unstated framework and helps to explain the anger aroused by lapses in spelling and grammar. Two letters specifically personify the English language, one claiming that the way 'so many Australians cold bloodedly murder English grammar makes me cringe' (13/11/84), the other that people who care about meanings 'care about words as individuals' (24/7/87). One article by the then Literary Editor, poet David Rowbotham, foreshadows, with the decline in literacy, the end of civilisation. The process is one of epic significance: 'Like a cloud containing thunder and lightening, there is a matter looming here that most of us, I think, would reckon as dramatically breathtaking'. He quotes a teacher who has declared that 'literacy has gone' and, while he himself 'hopes some day for a recovery of literacy and literature as one of the spiritual strengths of life', he is forced to agree that 'something is wrong with the word; and the death of the word will be the death of civilization, and the civility, that the world has known' (5/9/87). The alleged 'decline in literacy' becomes embroiled in an apocalyptic vision of the fate of the universe.

Linguistic variation and the appeal to authority

The literacy debate is underpinned by an intolerance of linguistic variation. Tolerance of such variation is 'permissiveness' and is contributing to the breakdown of authority. The standards of literacy debate is conflated with the notion of a single 'standard' correct English which is established by reference to traditional grammar and pronunciation dictionaries. Non-standard varieties or technically incorrect performances (as in poor spelling) are taken as signs of undesirable attitudes and personality traits.

Pronunciation is a burning issue for a significant minority, as with one letter writer who argues that public commentators 'should be pulled into line by someone in charge and obliged to peruse and conform to English (not American) dictionaries' (25/5/84), but in the literacy debate 'spelling' and 'grammar' are seen as most important.

Nine of the newspaper items call for, or report calls for, a return to teaching 'grammar' as a solution to perceived problems of literacy, including a report of the views of the Queensland Minister for Education. One item from an educational professional argues that there is no link between literacy and the explicit teaching of grammatical rules. In this respect, little has changed since the early twentieth century. Then too the calls for a 'return' to grammar were regularly voiced as were criticisms of its efficacy in teaching literacy. Two items from the debate in the *Queensland Educational Journal* which followed the modernisation of the elementary school curriculum in Queensland in 1904 can illustrate the point. A Mr. J. M. Broe complains to the editor that the 1904 issues of the *Journal* have been in 'high glee because parsing and analysis are doomed' and refers to the 'spirit of Vandalism' of educational reformers. He argues:

'To throw aside parsing and analysis, the basis, the body and soul of any language ever spoken by civilized people, in the vain hope of teaching children to speak properly, by correcting them now and again in a desultory kind of way, or by advising them to copy from their parents, seems to me like building castles, not in the sand, but right out in the water.' (Broe, 1905, p 19)

The editor, in reply, refers to the 'despotic regime of analysis and parsing' which happily has passed and argues:

'how (was it that) the masters of English prose and poetry gained the power to use the language with such beauty and magic force? Was it by a close study of analysis and parsing, as we have them in our primary schools? Clearly not.' (*Queensland Educational Journal*, April, 1905, p 3)

The continuity between the debate in 1905 and the contemporary debate is remarkable.

The associations of illiteracy

The dominant way of representing illiteracy or imperfect literacy is as a disease or disability – a stigma which is associated with fear, charity, unemployment and crime. The church is providing 'drought relief to Africa and literacy classes and aid to the landless poor in India' (10/12/84). 'Illiterate people are usually unemployed and unemployable ... as a result they often turned to crime' (27/12/84). Prisoners are 'sentenced' to courses in literacy (28/8/86). Telecom plans to give a rebate to 'the blind, illiterate and handicapped' (12/6/87). We are faced with a 'plague of illiteracy' (5/9/87). There are 'distraught parents shouting for help but not being heard' as 'teachers ... are finding more and more children with learning difficulties' (6/8/87). The illiterate go through life 'under-employed and ashamed' (25/5/87). They would not ask for information at libraries 'because the threat of humiliation frightened them' (29/8/84) and were unable to borrow recorded versions of books in State libraries unless they could obtain 'doctors' certificates saying that they were blind or partly-blind' (21/5/87).

Decline and fall and back to the basics

The vast majority of the 110 stories involving literacy present it as a problem which needs to be addressed. It is 'news' because it is a problem.

Sometimes this problem status is muted, merely an unstated assumption, as in straightforward descriptions of International Literacy Day activities, or of Adult Literacy Programmes; at others the presentation verges on panic. The spectre of 'decline' and the idea that 'something is terribly wrong' is conjured up in 37 items while only 11 dispute the decline notion or attempt to defuse the crisis mentality. One story emanating from a National Party Branch – the National Party is the most conservative of Australia's major political parties – suggests that there has been a 'massive cover up' about the decline. Allegedly 70 per cent of first-year Technical and Further Education (TAFE) students failed a routine literacy test. TAFE officers were so shocked that they kept the results secret. The solution offered by this National

Party Branch was to disband the Education Department and re-organise it along 'private lines' (2/5/85).

The stories of decline usually emanate from un-named business-men (a standard formula as utilised by one letter-writer reads, 'Businessmen have told me of being unable to hire a young girl competent enough to write names and answer the phone' 31/12/84), business organisations (according to a spokesperson for the Australian Chamber of Commerce, 'Many businessmen express concern at the basic literacy skills of school leavers' 12/11/85), university sources (there is a 'growing concern among academics that literacy skills have declined sharply' 17/4/84), politicians (the Liberals adopt a 'back to the basics' education policy 8/10/86), concerned parents ('The multiplying effect of the lowering of standards must be reversed before it is too late' 20/3/86), and newspaper editors ('the fact that nearly a million Australians are illiterate in English should make educational authorities every-where hang their heads in collective shame' 18/12/84). This for-midable array tends to overwhelm the teachers' representatives and educational researchers that defend the education system and present the evidence of studies disputing the decline theory.

The blame for 'decline' is most often attributed to teachers, though the mass media, popular culture, and 'new technology' are also culpable. TV comperes and sports commentators are blamed. In TV football commentaries, laments an editorial, 'often, ordin-ary rules of grammar seem not to apply; more infinitives are split than eyebrows in a football match' (12/5/87). For the head of universities in the US southern state of Georgia 'rock music and television are the basic causes of society's literacy problems' (22/2/84). It is a measure of the newsworthiness of the literacy issue, incidentally, that this last story emanating from Atlanta via Associated Press with no connection with Australia found its way into the *Courier-Mail*.

The consequences of decline are alarming. Not just unemploy-ment but the very destruction of society: 'The prospect of technol-ogy replacing the need for people to learn to read and write will threaten the structure of society' (26/8/85) and 'the death of the word will be the death of civilization' (5/9/87).

The way to retrieve the situation, in the narrative of decline, is to go back – 'back to the basics' – back to the discipline of grammar and drill, back for a 'recovery of literacy as one of the spiritual strengths of life' (5/9/87).

Literacy and the media

The discourse of literacy in the media is dominated by images of decline and crisis. Literacy is not seen as merely a technical skill but as an index of the 'health of society'. The literacy issue is the site upon which a whole variety of personal and societal prejudices are played out. The issue often functions as a vanguard for a much wider conservative agenda.

While the press reporting clearly reflects the political and community debate – most of the stories report actual statements by individuals – it is pertinent to point out that news values mediate the selection and presentation of the material. The media presentation of literacy is inflected by the criteria of news-worthiness – human interest, conflict, the extreme, the unusual, involving celebrities and political figures.

The reasoned statements of educational researchers reporting on studies which show that there is in fact no evidence of decline are largely lost in the face of these patterns of representation. This supports the findings of Johnson (1980, pp 80–85) who analysed the way in which the literacy debate was orchestrated in an *ABC Monday Conference* programme in 1978. The 'apparent rationality' of the debate – speaker for 'decline', speaker against, audience equally divided, 'neutral' compere, 'balanced' presentation – ensured the perpetration of the image of the literacy issue as a reasoned argument. In fact the use of 'scientific reports' by the President of the Australian Teachers' Federation to argue against the decline theory had little chance against the now legitimated anecdotal evidence and suggestive images of the proponent of the decline theory (Professor Harry Messel of the University of Sydney) who linked 'attitudes of society towards law, order, discipline and so forth' with allegedly disastrous changes in the educational system.

As 'literacy' becomes 'news' it is structured in terms of 'news-worthy' patterns including the familiar images of crisis and decline. New material is subsumed into these patterns and they seem to develop a life of their own which resists the interventions of rational debate. The media propagate and mobilise acceptance of these dominant patterns of representations. Those of us who have a professional interest in literacy issues must take cognisance of those patterns, if only to ensure that we are not trapped by them ourselves. In an environment where, within popular discourse, decline is casually assumed, it may be tempting to allow this as a proper framework for debate, ie allow the central question to become whether there has been decline or not. Yet surely the important question is not whether or not there has been decline but whether current standards are adequate to contemporary needs.

An analysis of the popular discourse of literacy alerts us to the fact that while such questions as 'decline' may appear to professionals to be empirically resolvable – ie a matter of measurement in popular discourse – they invoke attitudes and perceptions which operate at the level of social mythology.

References

Broe, J. M. (1905) A grammar point, a Grammar point. *Queensland Education Journal*, April, pp 18–19.

Donald, J. (1983) How illiteracy became a problem (and literacy stopped being one). *Journal of Education*, 165:1, pp 35–52.

Ewart, D. (1906) Report of the Director of Education in 'Thirtieth Annual Report of the Secretary for Public Instruction in Queensland ... 1905'. *Queensland Parliamentary Papers*, vol 1, pp 1311–1425.

Johnson, L. (1980) The media, the state and the educational standards debate. *The Australian and New Zealand Journal of Sociology*, 16:3, pp 80–85.

Keeves, J. D. & Bourke, S. F. (1976) *Australian studies in school performance: literacy and numeracy in Australian schools: a first report*. Canberra: Australian Government Publishing Service.

Little, G. (1978) Standards. *English in Australia*, 46, pp 3–13.

—— (1985) There is no decline. *Curriculum Development in Australian Schools*, 1, pp 4–7.

Parkin, A. (1984) 'Back to Basics' and the politics of education: competency testing in Australia and the United States. *Politics*, 19:2, pp 54–70.

Queensland Education Journal, April, 1905 (The doom of parsing and analysis) pp 3–4.

Samuel, P. (1976) Australia's educational scandal: we're turning out millions of dunces. *The Bulletin*, 15 May, pp 30–32.

Street, B. V. (1984) *Literacy in theory and practice*. Cambridge: Cambridge University Press.

6 Language, communication and reading

Asher Cashdan

Introduction

It does not seem as strange to me as to some of my colleagues that, having moved from work in education some years ago to a Department of Communication Studies, I should now be returning to education. For me, communication – and mostly this means through the medium of language – is the central core of everything that we do in education.

I mean this in two senses. First, that most of what education is doing is transmitting the culture, the ways of thinking and behaving, of previous and earlier generations, to the current younger one. That transmission is clearly a matter of communication both directly by spoken advice, instruction and admonition and indirectly (but still as communication) by example, and by a whole array of non-linguistic devices, including gesture, posture and all the rest. Second, education, and we emphasise this particularly in the early years, is about learning specific communication skills, most obviously those of reception and expression – listening and reading, talking and writing.

Knowing the ABC

In common parlance, education starts with the ABC. Yet among the many contradictions in our teaching is the long-standing refusal to teach children the actual letters of the alphabet. 'Look-and-say' exemplifies the common denial of access to knowledge that we practise on our pupils. Yet knowing the ABC enables children to organise the multiple grapheme-phoneme correspondences which form the core of the reading system – and this despite the many apparent inconsistencies in our orthography. Knowing the alphabet also makes it easier to write; it is sometimes forgotten even by reading specialists that writing and reading are learned at roughly the same time!

Why, then, do we hesitate to offer pupils essential knowledge? This chapter will argue that there are two strands to the answer. On the one hand is a theory of learning, both implicit and explicit and largely misguided; on the other is a complex of political and social factors which are particularly significant at the present time. It is to the latter that I should now like to turn.

The British educational revolution

Since 1988 we have had in Britain a major Education Reform Act, the establishment of a Curriculum Council to oversee the design and implementation of virtually the whole of the school curriculum and, within the language sphere alone, the publication of over half a dozen major reports and Government advisory papers. Without attempting a detailed analysis, we should nevertheless pause and ask what this activity is trying to achieve in the way of social engineering – and why.

Parenthetically, it is worth noting that such social engineering is far from new and far from always being progressive. Within this volume itself we may look at the paper by Putnis which refers to education inspectors' doubts about encouraging universal literacy in turn of the century Australia.

No conspiracy is being suggested: education never can, or should, be value-free. Moreover, much of social education and value formation is indirect and outside the classroom. The role of the media is obvious: *Dallas* purveys its values indirectly; the older *Star Trek* is nearer to Virgil's *Aeneid* (both of which, in their respective contexts, are about empire and the inculcation of colonial paternalism!).

In present-day Britain, I would suggest, there is an attempt to convince the rising generation that our complex, technology-oriented, capitalist society will thrive on a strong commitment to industrial/business values and technician skills – though the level of technicians needed is somewhat unclear. This is not just an issue for Britain; a global restructuring is in fact in progress. Even the Russian system now seems to feel the need to move in a similar direction.

Education for failure

At the same time as this reorientation of values – in effect a pressure towards a more pragmatic, utilitarian education with a high technology bias – is a dissatisfaction with the current operation of our education system. Government is not happy with the degree of delegation of the educational system, where there is considerable freedom, not just in LEA or school, but right down to the individual teacher. This is seen to be unsatisfactory because it leads to inconsistent and uneven educational practice and because, frankly, not all teachers have both the personal skills and the training to operate effectively in quite so independent a mode.

In its turn, this is closely linked with an educational ladder system which seems designed to fail, at some stage, all but a tiny handful of Oxbridge graduates, many of whom become the top civil servants, writing Education Acts and regarding teachers as minor functionaries!

This may sound like a joke (or be dismissed as jealousy), but there is a serious point here. Teachers, like most professionals and nearly all of the rest of the working population, see themselves as having failed at one stage or another of the educational ladder system. It takes some time to achieve rehabilitation and to acquire genuine confidence, without defensiveness, in one's abilities as a teacher. Yet, at the same time, we expect our teachers to achieve the near impossible. For instance, in the nursery/infant stage, teachers are supposed to have both the theoretical background and the intuitive skill to assess the exact point their children have reached in their intellectual growth, largely through play, and to intervene delicately to move them on to the next stage. This follows McV Hunt's (1969) theory of the match – setting the gap between where the learner is and where the learner should attempt to be at just the right size (like adjusting the points in a motor-car engine). In practice, though few are willing to admit this, these ideals are almost never reached. (This has been well documented in a series of classroom researches in the nursery school, including our own – see Cashdan, 1988.)

In recent years, we seem to have become more sophisticated about this problem and more aware of the crucial importance of analysing the interaction in the classroom between teacher and pupil. Yet we are doing little about this – and the newer trends in teacher education, while rightly focusing on the teacher's subject knowledge, at the same time devalue educational theory (much of which was dead wood anyway). They also pay too little attention to applied pedagogical training, often putting the most important interactions in the training process – including the supervision of teaching practice – into the hands of part-timers and untrained class teachers.

The centralised curriculum

Although there were some precursors of this, 1988 marked a major change in direction, in that Government intervened in the delegation of education and assumed a far greater degree of central control. This central control is being pursued to serve a number of ends. Among these one may discern at least the following:

1 At administrative level, central control from Whitehall is preferred (as in other areas than education) to delegation to local authority level.
2 Greater supervision from the centre will, it is hoped, lead to greater efficiency – in short, to saving money.
3 It is thought that a controlled curriculum, where there are national standards and programmes of study, coupled with national assessment practices, will guarantee standards to a much greater extent than in the past. At the same time, this makes possible a higher degree of ideological control from the government of the day, at least in broad terms (eg the reduction in sociology teaching!).
4 High visible performance standards can be achieved within a specified, deliberately-narrowed curriculum.

Grammar

The Secretary of State at the time of the Education Reform Act in 1988, saw salvation in the language field in the explicit teaching of grammar, including clause analysis, in error-free writing and in the promotion of Standard English. These concerns are echoed, with varying emphasis, in the curriculum documents that have been reaching us in the last two years. In the most recent consolidated one (DES, June 1989 – generally known as the Second Cox

Report) it is interesting to see that many of these concerns have been expressed in much more liberal and less confining ways than the Secretary of State might have expected. What seems to have happened is that the curriculum experts who worked with Professor Cox succeeded in convincing him that less direct methods of teaching might, in the longer run, bear better fruit with most pupils.

The argument for grammar in some form is not just that it is a good thing in itself; as we argued in discussing the ABC earlier, grammar serves as an organiser for language, promoting understanding of language (and knowledge more generally) – in other words, promoting insights by making structures explicit. But as teachers know, the mere offer of a structure can simply become more inert knowledge. Even superficial studies of Piaget have helped the current generation of teachers to appreciate that learning by rote does not lead to understanding and application unless the pupil has the prerequisite sub-structures. In other words, the direct teaching of grammar could be largely a waste of time and would by the same token be boring and discouraging for pupils.

But there is a tension here. Despite the enthusiasm of those who would have pupils learn incidentally, in context, while pursuing worthwhile activities, such approaches do not guarantee success; nor do they liberate the learner to be in charge of their own learning processes.

Doing the right thing for the wrong reason

It seems to me, then, that the ex-Secretary of State and his followers are in fact right to ask that pupils be given an explicit structured context and vocabulary for their learning, whether this be the ABC or the vocabulary of grammar. Where they are wrong is in thinking that this can be done easily and unproblematically and that it can be achieved with no risks early in the school career of the pupil. There are many complexities to sort out. Let me take two 'case studies' to help to make the point.

1   Correcting pupils' mistakes

A persistent educational dilemma is deciding how far to hold up the learner's developing understanding by niggling correction of minor mistakes. This is especially interesting in reading and writing, where the high redundancy of language means that much correction is not necessary for successful communication. In fact, we can only correct others because we know what they are trying to say! When the pupil writes 'would of' it hardly matters in communication terms; in fact some would argue that such an expression is part of the evolution of language and that once most people are writing 'would of' this becomes a correct expression. Leaving this unconvincing argument aside on the grounds that one should always resist 'mistakes' which reduce insight into the language, its history and its orthography, it is nevertheless true that much correction does illustrate little more than the success of the communication to the teacher. As Ernest Gellner (1981) points out, in discussing anthropological field studies, no anthropologists return saying 'we could not understand their culture, their kinship patterns, etc' – in fact, rightly or wrongly, we work them out quite quickly!

So it could be argued that much classroom correction, particularly of pupils' writing, is unnecessary. At the same time, learning in context at an intuitive level has also been attacked. Most recently, for example, Littlefair (1989), following the work of Halliday and Martin, argues that pupils not only need to use and understand a range of genres in writing – narrative, expository, persuasive, etc – but they also need to be taught their linguistic features quite explicitly.

So Case Study 1 suggests that teachers need to exercise constant judgement in where to correct and where to leave alone. At one extreme, creativity will be stifled and interest killed; at the other, systematic structures will not be learned and the pupil will both lack control over the learning process and have no ability to self-correct.

It may be, too, that the reason why most adults nowadays are such poor spellers is largely because of the non-insightful way in which they encountered English orthography through Schonell-inspired 'look-and-say' methods of learning to read.

2   Metacognition and reading difficulties

A colleague and I (Cashdan and Wright, 1990) have been working recently with nine-year-old children who are behind in their reading. We are working with a long-standing hypothesis that they will be particularly helped by skill-based methods, in particular by the emphasis on phonology recently revived by Bryant and Bradley (1985). Our emphasis is on sounding, rhyming, letter-play. We see these as developing more insight than visual methods into the nature of the reading and writing systems. We have discovered in our study that these children even at the age of nine have little knowledge of what is a sentence, a word, a letter, nor of how they function. Perhaps they were told these things too early, as rote information (as some educational politicians are now arguing that they should be) with no context to support their understanding. More likely, perhaps, they were never given this kind of structural vocabulary at all. Either way, we have found that with careful analysis and teaching we can now supply this 'metacognitive' understanding and that this is likely to lead to re-motivation and to improved ability to read and write effectively (see Wright and Cashdan, 1989).

Process-based instruction and a not-very-new approach to pedagogy

A major lesson of this chapter has been that we need to emphasise pedagogy much more – the meeting of art and science in the classroom. Most of the decisions about when to offer structure explicitly, what vocabulary of learning to give to the pupil and when to withhold such contextual information in the interest of getting on with the task in hand without interruption, are a matter for the teacher's judgement in the live situation. I would only add that if in any doubt one should always offer the learner the tools. If the offer is premature, it will not be taken up; but no harm will be done, provided that the offer is genuinely an offer and not an insistence on rote learning. One recent impressive working out of the classroom process is to be found in the Special Needs work of Ashman and Conway (1989) and their Process-based Instruction. On a foundation of cognitive psychological theory, they follow through from the initial task analysis by the pupil, to an examination of the skills at the pupil's disposal, the strategies that will be needed, through to the outcomes and their evaluation before re-commencing the cycle. Crucially, the planning, analysis and assessment/generalisation are in the pupils' hands, so that they are in charge of their own learning. Though based in special needs work, the analysis is generalisable to most spheres of education.

We need to offer pupils the opportunity to acquire knowledge and the structures to carry it and we need to work this out in the theatre of action, in the classroom. As a teacher-educator, I see it as essential that both I and my colleagues be able and willing to demonstrate this in the classroom ourselves, working with our own students. If for any reason that becomes less possible, then we will have failed as trainers and Merritt (1986 and elsewhere) will be justified in his frequently reiterated claim that teacher-trainers who cannot exemplify their theories do more harm than good.

Finally, it is inevitable that this has been a political argument – education *is* a political activity. It is also one about text and subtext. The second Cox Report (DES, June 1989) to which I referred above, is surprisingly enlightened at times considering its origins. There is much heartening encouragement of valuable educational practices – broad experiences for pupils in a wide range of contexts and no endorsement of rote learning. Indeed at times it goes too far: why, for instance, should there be no assessment of knowledge of language terminology except in context? It seems quite legitimate to me to ask pupils to demonstrate significant knowledge directly. But what is most important to stress is that there *is* ongoing struggle over educational aims and methods. As teachers we should welcome this, engage in it and never pretend that politics can be kept out of education. If we do, we shall not be keeping them out, only allowing them to dictate our practice at a less conscious level!

References

Ashman, A. F. and Conway, R. N. F. (1989) *Cognitive strategies for special education: Process-based instruction*. London: Routledge.

Bryant, P. and Bradley, L. (1985) *Children's reading problems: psychology and education*. Oxford: Basil Blackwell.

Cashdan, A. (1988) The dialogue approach: tutorial teaching. In Cashdan, A. and Meadows, S. *Helping children learn*. Oxford: Basil Blackwell.

Cashdan, A. and Wright, J. (1990) Intervention strategies for backward readers in the primary school classroom. In *Children's difficulties in reading, writing and spelling: challenges and responses*, ed P. D. Pumfrey and C. D. Elliott, Lewes: Falmer Press.

DES (June 1989) *English for ages 5 to 16*. Proposals of the Secretary of State for Education and Science and the Secretary of State for Wales. London: HMSO.

Gellner, E. (1981) General introduction: relativism and universals. In *Universals of human thought*, ed B. Lloyd and J. Gay, Cambridge: Cambridge University Press.

Littlefair, A. B. (1989) Register awareness: an important factor in children's continuing reading development, *Reading*, *23*, 56–61.

Merritt, J. E. (1986) What's wrong with teaching reading? In *Literacy: Teaching and learning language skills*, ed A Cashdan, Oxford: Basil Blackwell.

Putnis, P. [Chapter in this Volume]

Wright, J. and Cashdan, A. (1989) Teaching children with reading difficulties: metacognitive aspects. UKRA Annual Conference, Ormskirk.

7   Text-processing with the computer: the implications for literacy

David Wray

Introduction

Of all the various ways in which the microcomputer can be used to develop children's language and literacy, word processing and desk top publishing have perhaps received most attention (Maxted, 1988; Wray & Medwell, 1989a). This attention has been focused largely upon how the new medium of the computer can enhance children's writing. Little attention has been given to the effects of using the computer upon children's perceptions of literacy, and upon the nature of literacy itself. It is these questions which will be discussed in this chapter.

The chapter begins with a brief discussion on the nature of literacy as presently conceived. I will then go on to outline some of the features and benefits of text-processing with the computer. In the final section I will examine the impact of text-processing upon the process of literacy. Throughout the chapter the term 'text-processing' is used to mean all aspects of creating and manipulating a text on a computer, that is, a combination of word processing and desk top publishing.

What is literacy?

As a brief exploration of the nature of literacy, this section centres around three quotations taken from de Castell, Luke and Egan (1986), each of which highlight a different focus for a definition of literacy. These three foci embody distinct types of views about literacy, each of which has its contemporary adherents as well as historical significance.

1   Literacy as culture

'The classical definition of literacy as embracing the domain of high culture fails to address our situation, and we no longer accept its implicit associations linking literacy with an esoteric lettered class.' (de Castell et al, 1986, p 7)

In our everyday use of language we commonly use the term 'literate' in similar ways to 'educated' or 'cultured'. We might say things like 'These children come from highly literate home backgrounds', or 'This man is extremely literate. He seems to have read everything'. The term here means more than simply reading and writing, but has implications of some kind of quality.

This usage stems from the historical development of literacy. We are so accustomed nowadays to literacy being a more or less universal phenomenon that it is difficult to appreciate that for hundreds of years it was not. Before the invention of the printing press, literacy was very much the preserve of an elite. The position of scribe was one with a high degree of status because the skills it demanded were in short supply. Reading and writing were not skills possessed by the majority of the population, but were concentrated in certain groups. Religious groups used them to preserve and embellish sacred works. Other written materials, because they were painstaking to produce, were scarce and expensive and therefore the preserve of those with sufficient resources.

This elitist view of literacy was, in fact, vigorously upheld by some groups who saw it as positively harmful for ordinary people to be 'taught their letters'. If they could read, they could then read works such as the Bible for themselves, and then would not need the church to interpret it for them. The universalisation of literacy, through the spread of printing, was for many people a highly political process.

The effect of the introduction of printing was to make the elitist view of literacy increasingly untenable. The more people had reading and writing available to them, the more they came to involve themselves in it, and in the end rely upon it. The spread of literacy made for a more complex society which, in turn, demanded greater mastery of literacy. Universal literacy became essential for the effective functioning of society. One of the chief motivating forces behind universal education was the need for literate workers. The three Rs were given the central position in education that they have occupied ever since. In more recent times the degree of literacy in a country has come to be a measure of the civilisation of that country. Revolutions in countries such as Russia, China and Cuba have had as one of their chief aims the spread of literacy. Literacy is no longer elitist but universal.

2   *Literacy and citizenship*

'A person is literate when he has acquired the essential knowledge and skills which enable him to engage in all those activities in which literacy is required for effective functioning in his group or community.' (de Castell et al, 1986, p 8.)

As I have just argued, modern society needs people with sufficient command of literacy to act as good and useful citizens. Citizenship involves a number of roles, for each of which literacy is essential. Heath (1983), in her research into the experience of literacy of selected American communities, found literacy being used for seven socially orientated purposes.

   i   *Instrumental* Literacy provided information about the practical problems of everyday life, eg bills, traffic signs, price tickets.

   ii   *Social interactional* Literacy provided information needed to maintain social relationships, eg letters, cards, cartoons.

   iii   *News related* Literacy provided information about distant events, eg newspapers, newsletters.

   iv   *Memory-supportive* Literacy served as an aid to memory, eg notes, telephone directories, address books.

   v   *Substitutes for oral messages* Literacy was used when direct oral contact was impossible, eg messages, notes to school.

   vi   *Provision of permanent record* Literacy was used when records were required for legal purposes, eg tax forms, certificates.

   vii   *Confirmation* Literacy provided support for ideas already held, eg settling disagreements, checking against recipes.

Although these uses of literacy are rather different from those envisaged by other definers of 'functional literacy', they still reflect the basic premise of this view: literacy is a tool which supports effective functioning as a citizen.

3 Literacy and self-determination

'Being "literate" has always referred to having mastery over the process by means of which culturally significant information is coded.' (de Castell et al, 1986, p 88.)

Of course, the idea that a person needs to be literate in order to be a good citizen is subject to the very powerful criticism that it sees literacy as an essentially passive thing. If individuals are thought of as existing to serve society's needs and to fit in with its demands, literacy can be seen as one device for controlling them. This concept is central to the work on literacy of Paulo Freire and his associates (Freire, 1972). Literacy is, according to Freire, predominantly used as a mechanism of social control. Those agencies in society which seek to control others, either governments, companies or other associations, in fact require certain minimal levels of literacy in those they control. The mechanisms of social control in modern society depend upon literacy. Propaganda, rules, regulations, publicity of various forms all use print and depend upon the population's ability to decipher that print.

Literacy, however, can be defined as involving much more than this passive approach. The third definition of literacy claims that it involves 'having mastery over the process by means of which culturally significant information is coded'. If this is accepted it implies that the literate person, far from being controlled by the manifestations of literacy, is, in fact, in control of them. This involves having some autonomy in the process of using literacy, and having the ability to make choices (Wray, 1988). Propaganda and publicity rely for their effect upon recipients' lack of autonomy, and their sometimes overpowering influence upon the choices made. The concepts of autonomy and control are, therefore, central to literacy. Later in this chapter I shall argue that autonomy and control are precisely the things which are increased by the use of the computer for text-processing. Firstly, however, I shall outline briefly the impact which text-processing can have upon children's writing. This is explored more fully elsewhere (Wray and Medwell, 1989b).

The impact of text-processing

Commentators seem to agree that word processing is an enabling device for children's writing. Perhaps its most obvious advantage is that it is almost guaranteed to produce instant success for its users. All writing produced on the computer, whatever its quality, 'looks good'. The computer does not allow differentiation between those with well and poorly developed physical writing skills. Because word-processed text has a professional physical appearance, this is an immediate and important step towards its goal of effective communication.

This in itself would not, of course, be sufficient reason for encouraging children to use the computer to write. Many teachers have also found that word processing leads to an improved quality in children's writing. Editing and revising texts is made much simpler when it can be done on the screen before committing the writing to paper. This decrease of physical effort encourages children to edit and revise, with consequent improvement in content, style and clarity. By using the computer, all writing becomes provisional and open to addition, extension, rearrangement, deletion and reshaping. This fact cannot help but have profound implications for children's perceptions of the process of writing and its products.

Desk top publishing goes further than simple word processing in terms of the facilities it provides for writers. It allows children to produce their writing in formats which are 'realistic' in the sense that they correspond to formats the children regularly encounter in the outside world, for example, newspapers and magazines. It is easy to underestimate the level of children's awareness of these formats. Given access to software which is supposed to allow them to produce newspapers, for example, they often complain unexpectedly about quite small deviations, such as type-face and layout, thus indicating a surprising sensitivity.

The desk top publishing environment has some features which make it particularly useful for realistic writing formats. One of the most important of these is the cut and paste facility. By using this, sections of pages can be electronically lifted from one place and moved or copied to another. This is an extension of the provisionality of writing mentioned earlier. Anything children produce can always be changed in a number of ways, not only in content but also in layout. Using the computer means, of course, that they can experiment with several layouts before finally committing themselves to one.

Another feature which desk top publishing makes possible is the mixing of text and pictures. Software is available which enables users to snatch pictures from video players and cameras, or to scan in photographs or diagrams. These pictures are then digitised and imported into the desk top publishing environment. Once under the control of the computer software, the pictures can be manipulated in various ways: stretched, enlarged, reduced, rotated, reversed, chopped into pieces and overlaid or interspersed with text. This is a facility of immense potential, which enables users of small personal computers to produce pages which are almost indistinguishable from those of real newspapers. It extends provisionality and gives the writer increased power over the product.

There are two major implications from the use of word processing and desk top publishing which deserve fuller explanation.

1 Provisionality of text

Because text on a computer is easily reshapeable, in content and format, it becomes provisional. Words and sentences can be altered as can the place at which those words and sentences occur. Not only that but the physical appearance of a page of text can also be changed. The type-faces, the size of margins, the number of columns, the number and position of pictures are all open to alteration: alteration which can be effected by pressing a few keys. This simplicity encourages, in fact almost forces, the writer to reflect on his/her product. The presence of alternatives implies choice and the ability to choose implies the writer having control over the process.

2 Control

Text-processing puts the writer in control of the writing process. Decisions have to be made, and alternatives selected. The final product is not arbitrarily forced upon the writer by the size of the paper being written on, the width of the lines, the size of the margins, the size of the picture already drawn etc. These things are under the control of the writer, and again the need to make decisions about them forces reflectiveness in the writer.

The implications for literacy

What are the effects of these new facilities upon children's perceptions of literacy and the nature of literacy itself? There seem to be three major issues.

1   Text as servant

When using desk top publishing the writer gains control over text and can shape it any way he/she wishes. The writer thus has 'mastery' over the text, in the words of our earlier definition of literacy, in a more complete sense than is usually the case. Notice that this relationship between literate person and text is the opposite to that more commonly found. In many of our dealings with text in the world, it is text which controls us rather than vice versa. Text (or print) tells us how to run our lives, and tries to persuade us (with a great deal of success) what to buy, what to do and what to think. The reversal of this relationship which comes into operation with text-processing seems likely to challenge perceptions of text.

2   Writing can control

A further dimension to this comes into play when we consider the kinds of texts which are most often produced on the computer. These tend to be public in nature and to be produced with the express purpose of affecting other people. Children use desk top publishing most often to produce newspapers, posters, and advertisements, all of which contain writing aimed at influencing others' actions. Having this aim, they are forced to consider how such writing goes about influencing others. In attempting to achieve this influence in their own work, they are likely to become more aware of the strategies which are employed in the real world to achieve it. And this increased awareness is in turn likely to lead to an increased ability to resist being influenced themselves. Learning to use writing to control others may enable children to resist others' attempts to control them.

3   Presentation enhances power

A common phrase often employed in debates about secrecy is 'Information is power', and certainly the possession of information which others do not have does give a distinct advantage. There is a sense, though, in which power does not reside only in the possession of information, but also in how this is presented. The washing powder produced by a small firm may actually be superior to that produced by a multi-national giant, and have the research data to prove it, but still fail to sell as well because of the superior advertising campaign of its rival. In other words, it is the way in which information is presented that produces the major effect.

Now one of the main ways in which the advent of desk top publishing has revolutionised information-presentation is the facility it gives to anybody with access to readily available equipment to produce print-outs which rival those produced professionally. In the same way that word processing liberates the child with poor handwriting from the limitations of this disability, desk top publishing liberates the amateur computer user from the limitations of lack of professional resources. In theory, with desk top publishing, there need be little difference between the presentation of a multi-national company and that of a primary school. It is perhaps true that at the moment the requisite hardware is a little beyond the resources of a primary school, but this is likely to be a temporary phenomenon. Even now, £7000 or £8000 will purchase a system which will produce black and white material of equal quality to that produced by most professional publishers. This price is certain to reduce in real terms, and new facilities will be available in the near future.

This situation implies a real democratisation of literacy. Groups previously unable to compete in terms of presentation can now, by combining resources, produce materials which gain greatly in credibility by their professional appearance. Achieving this appearance becomes a central skill in literacy: 'having mastery over the process by which culturally significant information is coded'. Thus the spread of desk top publishing not only alters users' perceptions of literacy, but also extends the nature of literacy itself.

Such a situation, of course, has profound implications. Increased control over the presentation of information may be liberating in some circumstances, but it may also be liberty-threatening. With the new provisionality of text and page, the concept of the 'definitive record' may become somewhat blurred. This record can always be altered. Rewriting history may require no more than the pressing of a few keys on a computer. It is clear that, in this Orwellian world, controls are going to be increasingly necessary. The key question, of course, is who will do the controlling. And who will control them?

Conclusion

There can be little doubt that the use of text-processing is both a political and a politicising process. The manipulation of information to serve particular ends can fulfil political goals, but can also raise awareness of the ways in which information can be manipulated. The ability to engage in these processes is, for the first time, becoming available to all.

It may seem extreme to argue that the use of text-processing with young children is a political process. This, however, ignores the fact that literacy, at any level, has never been politically neutral. As developers and cultivators of literacy, teachers need to be aware of the implications of what they are doing. The main thrust of this chapter has been to argue that the potential of text-processing changes these implications in significant ways.

References

de Castell, S., Luke, A. & Egan, K. (1986) *Literacy, society and schooling*. Cambridge: Cambridge University Press.

Freire, P. (1972) *Pedagogy of the oppressed*. London: Penguin.

Heath, S. B. (1983) *Ways with words*. Cambridge: Cambridge University Press.

Maxted, D. (1988) *Getting into print*. Lincoln: Microelectronics Education Development Unit.

Wray, D. (1988) Censorship and literacy. *Reading*, 22, 2, pp 137–142.

Wray, D. & Medwell, J. (eds) (1989a) *Using desk-top publishing*. Ormskirk: United Kingdom Reading Association.

—— (1989b) Using desk-top publishing to develop literacy. *Reading*, 23, 2, pp 62–68.

8 We learn written language much as we learn spoken language . . . (for)

Jeff Hynds

In this article I shall propose the motion that we learn written language much as we learn spoken language. However, at the outset I must make it clear what I am *not* saying.

1 I am not saying that written language is the *same* as spoken language. It clearly differs, sometimes substantially, in various ways that we could specify, for example in choice of words or word order. ('Thou still unravished bride of quietness' is unlikely as a piece of everyday conversation.) This is an extensive matter in its own right which I have only time to summarise briefly here, as follows.

As we all know, writing is not just speech written down, or a derivative of speech. One of the most impressive and widely respected arguments for difference between spoken and written language has been that of the Canadian, David Olson, and his colleagues (Olson, 1977, 1984; Hildyard & Hidi, 1985; Chafe, 1985; Torrance & Olson, 1985). They have argued that written language has evolved into a form of language that is decontextualised and independent of its immediate surroundings, unlike speech. This argument has been followed by others, for example by Donaldson (1984, with Reid 1985, 1989). She suggests that written language is 'disembedded'.

However, this autonomous model of literacy has been challenged by a number of people (Labov, 1969; Stubbs, 1980), and most powerfully by Dr Brian Street at Sussex University (Street, 1984). Dr Street, taking a more international view, argues that the notion that written language is an autonomous, context-free, 'disembedded', explicit and universal form of language is an illusion.

It has been invented by certain groups to justify their own command of it. (Much the same idea is reflected in the work of Paulo Freire in the third world, cf. Freire and Macedo, 1987.) What is particularly significant in this respect is Street's analysis of Olson et al's *own* written language. Presumably this language should be the epitome of all that Olson, and indeed Donaldson, claim for written language. Their writing ought to provide us with a first class example of context-free disembeddedness. But ironically and rather amusingly Street demonstrates that:

'much of their own writing is embedded, context-laden and ethnocentric ... They represent the classic disproof of their own claims for the detached and context-free qualities of writing. What they are writing about in reality are the ideal standards of their own social group, those that give meaning to their work ...' (Street, 1984)

For the truth is that there are many literacies, just as there are many oracies, and they are all embedded in their own particular social contexts or sub-cultures. And there are many ways to embed or contextualise language, spoken or written, not only by physical situations or paralinguistic features, but by socially acquired assumptions and attitudes, expectations and knowledge (eg the 'generic cues' of Cochran-Smith, 1984). Michael Rosen in his recent book *Did I hear you write?* shows how children draw on their learned culture in their orality and can do so in their writing. What is spoken and what is written share a common origin and feed off one another (Rosen, 1989).

It is simplistic to see hard and fast divisions between spoken and written language, as if there was only one kind of speaking and one kind of writing. There are many kinds and some are similar and some are different in varying degrees. And, yes, undoubtedly *some* forms of written language can have very different functions from some forms of spoken language. That I accept.

2   I am not saying that it is natural to learn written language and that it does not have to be taught. (I consider this to be an erroneous and rather romantic notion.) It is not natural and it does have to be taught. *We have to teach children to read and write.* However, I do not think *spoken* language is natural either, and *it also has to be taught.* When unfortunate children who have had no teachers have been found, like the wild boy of the Ardennes, or

Genie, whose father kept her isolated until she was 13 (Curtiss, 1977), they have acquired no language at all, spoken or written. Indeed, I would go further and say that everything has to be taught that is not a biologically inherited function, like crawling or walking, or sucking or screaming. Speaking is not a biologically inherited function, as Sapir pointed out long ago:

'The process of acquiring speech is, in sober fact, an utterly different sort of thing from the process of learning to walk.' (Sapir, 1921)

Genie could walk, but she could not talk. She had no one to teach her.

It is perhaps also worth pointing out that if speech were biologically inherited the world would not have developed thousands of different languages (only one), and human beings would be equipped with specific organs for the production of speech. As it is, our so-called speech organs are not speech organs at all, but eating and breathing organs which we have adapted, over some thousands of years, to an unnatural purpose, that of producing symbolic speech sounds.

So I am saying that *both spoken and written language are not natural and have to be taught if they are to be learned.*

Now I know that some people think that speaking *is* innate or natural. You don't have to be taught; you just pick it up. It is only *written language*, reading and writing, that is unnatural, and therefore, they say, it has to be taught. Donaldson's views about speaking and reading are not untypical:

'Children, as we all know, learn to speak and to understand speech without depending on systematic instruction. They start to do this spontaneously within the first eighteen months of life, given that they are spoken to in ordinary natural ways (which as a rule are not consciously planned). In these circumstances most children 'latch on' readily, and soon learn to make sense of the speech that is all around them ... When children learn to interpret speech they do not for the most part consciously attend to the words they hear. This is well established. They do not concern themselves with word meanings, but rather with a perception of the total meaning of utterances in context. We may say that for young children, an utterance is *embedded* in its context, is never considered apart from its context. And this embedding context includes, most importantly, what is seen as the purpose of the speaker. It is no exaggeration to say that children are concerned most of the time with what people mean, not with what words mean. Yet somehow – and this is a large part of what makes first language learning so remarkable and so intriguing – they learn enough about words at some level of consciousness to be able to put them together and express new meanings of their own.

So this is what children actually do as they learn spoken language. And at first they could do no other. It is the way human beings learn to speak. It does not follow that they can effectively learn to read in the same way.' (Donaldson, 1989)

I will pass over the vaguenesses and the contradictions of this extraordinary passage ('latch on' readily ... yet somehow ..., etc) to reiterate that such views are not uncommon. As we have seen they are Olsonesque, though Olson himself is cautious about any implications for teaching. Perera is somewhat bolder:

'It is clear, I think, that writing is not 'natural' in the way speech is. Speaking is as fundamental a part of being human as walking upright ... Learning to read and write is hard work.' (Perera, 1984)

It is perhaps surprising to find Perera, who has made distin- guished contributions to our understanding of spoken and written language (Perera, 1984, 1986, 1987), not only disagreeing with Sapir but being so categoric. Certainly people do seem to hold decided views on this matter. The most recent example I have encountered is, appropriately under the circumstances, included in the latest issue of the UKRA Journal. Here I read that:

'whereas language in its spoken (or manual) (*?sic*) form, is natural, reading and writing are artificial, manufactured activities. This means that our brains are pre-programmed to develop spoken language, but we have to adapt and apply a number of different cognitive and linguistic skills in order to learn to read and write.' (Stainthorp, 1989)

This is a confident claim (notwithstanding the unclear use of the word 'manual'), though like most such claims it remains quite unsubstantiated by the article in which it appears. Nevertheless such views are widespread and of long standing, and part of a set of beliefs about the learning of written language that have become traditional during the twentieth century. I now want to suggest (1) why I think these views are mistaken and (2) why I think they are believed and sustained.

1 Why is it mistaken to think spoken language is natural and written language is unnatural and hard work?

In the first place I believe that these views completely under-estimate the phenomenal amount of complex learning that children accomplish when they learn to talk, possibly because such large numbers of them do it so well that it has become common-place, and possibly because, unlike reading and writing, it is invisible.

Spoken language, as well as written language, is extensively rule-governed, and there is a great deal to learn. Children have to learn not only words and their variant forms (which they do at the rate of about twenty words a day), but rules of word order, rules for grammatical signalling, and phonemic rules. They have to learn, for example, which sounds are allophones of the same phoneme, and which are not; without this knowledge it is impos-sible to understand or produce speech; furthermore the situation is different in different languages. They must learn how all these combine to convey meaning. They must learn how the prosodic features of language, like stresses, pauses and intonations, inter-relate with, and leaven, this meaning. They must learn that mean-ings are not simply inherent in words, grammatical organisations or prosodic features, but also in the context of social interchange, and thus can be influenced, or even significantly altered, by para-linguistic signals such as gesture, facial expression or body lan-guage (all of which also have to be learned). They must learn, in any case, that meaning is frequently idiomatic as well as literal. There is much more than all this even. For example, speakers come to learn when and how to select and use particular language or particular implications for particular occasions. (Think of tact or sarcasm.) Learning the 'registers' of a language, those that speakers need to achieve 'communicative competence', is extreme-ly complex, let alone all the rest of it.

Indeed, if learning to read and write is 'hard work', then learn-ing spoken language must be even harder! Yet we find that many children have learnt an enormous amount of this language even by age 3 or 4, though certainly by no means all of it, and not necessarily all in equal measure (Bruner, 1984). Nevertheless, most will have achieved a substantial amount of complex language learning in all spoken departments, much of it when quite young, without any obvious hard work at all!

How do they do it? Well, they start early, well before the age of one, and they usually have quite good teaching from the beginning. This teaching comes from their parents, family, friends, from sundry practices consequent upon their social situation (eg going shopping, fetching water) and eventually, when they are old enough, from many of the activities they are involved in at school. In short, they learn spoken language *in use, in action, in true and total contexts,* by observing, imitating, hypothesising and experimenting, getting it wrong, getting it right, constantly being helped by various teachers.

In this article I am of course using the word 'teach' (and its associated forms 'teaching', 'taught') in the way commonly used by good teachers nowadays, meaning 'to cause learning', or more fully, 'to create the conditions that cause true learning' (cf. Lightfoot and Martin, 1988). There is otherwise no point in teaching. Several people have described the characteristics of this good teaching, and the conditions that are created. Holdaway (1979), for example, has described its emulative rather than instructional nature. Smith, in a definitive essay, has given us a penetrating analysis of the conditions that cause true learning (Smith, 1983).

These conditions are, of course, crucial, and the focus of my own work with teachers, for several years, has been to consider how we can practically create these same conditions in schools and classrooms. For teaching spoken language? No, I do it for teaching *written language!* You can't do that, says Donaldson, 'this may be the way human beings learn to speak, but it does not follow that they can effectively learn to read and write in the same way'. I believe they can, and that there's evidence to show that they can, and moreover I believe this way of learning is a paradigm for all learning, for all children in all situations. This is nothing new at all; it has always been so.

Do we learn written language like we learn spoken language? There is in fact nowadays considerable research evidence to show that we do, *when the conditions are the same for learning it.* Indeed, there is so much of this evidence that it would be impossible, in this short article, to investigate it all fully. Some of it has been reviewed by Nigel Hall in an excellent UKRA monograph (Hall,

1987). But, for the purposes of this debate, it will perhaps be clearest if I classify, with a brief synopsis of each, some 20 of the best known researches. I have followed this classification by looking, a little more fully, at a specific example of just one of the pieces of research from the list.

An attempted classification of some relevant research

A   CASE STUDIES (of individual children)

Bissex (1980, 1984)	Case study of her son Paul's writing and reading development from about 5 to 10, later compared with Scott from a less favoured background (1984).
Butler (1979)	Case study of Cushla's reading development from birth. Cushla was born handicapped and diagnosed as brain damaged.
Calkins (1983)	Susie was 8 at the beginning of this study of her writing development within a supportive and conducive classroom setting.
Fry (1985)	Case studies of six children aged 8 to 15 who saw themselves as readers.
Holdaway (1979)	Investigations of 'reading-like behaviour' revealed in children as young as 2.
Payton (1984)	A study, by her mother, of Cecilia's literacy development from about age 3 until just after entry into school.

B   INVESTIGATIONS OF GROUPS (either of random samples or groups specially selected. These investigations also involve case studies)

Clark (1976)	A now well-known study of 32 young fluent readers at age 5, and an examination of the circumstances that had brought this about.

Dombey (1983, 1988a, 1988b)

An investigation of the complex nature of early child-adult reading encounters. The children, all aged about 3 or 4, were from contrasting social backgrounds.

Fox (1983, 1986, 1988, 1989)

An analysis, over several years, of the spontaneous spoken narratives of five children (aged 3½– 6). An extensive corpus of some 43,000 words reveals the range of complex narrative and literary competences that these young children have already acquired.

Ferreiro and Teberosky (1983, 1984, 1985)

A renowned investigation of the literacy development of Argentinian children aged 4–6 from two contrasting situations (from middle and lower class social groups). The researchers also examined what happened to the children during the first years of schooling and 'came up with a devastating conclusion' (Moon 1985). Amongst other researches, Ferreiro has also studied slum and middle-class children in Mexico City with similar findings (1984).

Harste, Woodward and Burke (1984)

Extremely influential and highly informative award-winning research based on close observation of the literacy behaviour of children aged 3–6. Their conclusion: 'Written language is learned from the inside out in a socially supportive and conducive environment ... In the process of using written language, the child takes ownership of the written language learning process'.

Ingham (1982)	A 3-year investigation of about 30 children, all aged 10 at the beginning of the study, to discover why some had become *avid* readers and some *infrequent* readers. Part of the Bradford Book Flood experiment.
Newman (1984) and colleagues (ed 1985)	An examination of the writing of children aged 2 to 6 in the light of Harste et al's research, concluding with a case study of Shawn, a non-writer aged 6, during his first year in a supportive classroom. Also (ed 1985) a collection of papers, including some significant case studies, by Newman and colleagues on whole language and literacy learning.
Temple, Nathan, Burris and Temple (Revised, 1988)	A wide-ranging survey, drawing on research, of children's writing from their earliest days to their first years in school, with a discussion of classroom implications.
Wells (1985a, 1985b, 1986)	Wells has written extensively about the remarkable Bristol Language and Literacy Project. One of the most significant findings of the research was that children who heard written language read aloud and shared books in pre-school family situations were the most likely to develop as readers at school.

C   ETHNOGRAPHIC STUDIES (Groups in Social Contexts)

Cochran-Smith (1984)	How 'adults in one setting ... socialize their children into particular patterns of literacy by helping them develop the literary and social knowledge needed to use and understand print'.
Goelman, Oberg and Smith (1984)	Record of an international symposium held at the University of Victoria, B.C. Several of the participants reported on the development of literacy in particular social situations.
Heath (1982, 1983)	A comparative study of the development of language and literacy in three contrasting communities in the south-eastern United States. Each community generated its own form of literacy as part of its own sub-cultural behaviour pattern.
Taylor (1983)	A comparative study of the growth of literacy in six families, showing strong social learning taking place.

D   INVESTIGATIONS OF PARTICULAR FEATURES

Read (1986) see also Bissex (1980) and Temple et al (1988) above	Read demonstrates the sensitive and logical ways in which children set about learning to spell.
Calkins (1980)	About children learning punctuation in the context of using it.
Cazden, Cordeiro and Giocobbe (1985)	Similar to the above. Learning punctuation in action.

An example from the work of Carol Fox

Dr Fox has been studying the spontaneous oral narratives of children aged 3½–6. These were children who had experienced readings and sharings of books by a variety of children's writers such as Eric Carle, and Janet and Allan Ahlberg. Often these children had many such experiences in the course of a year, including repeated re-readings of favourite books. From these children Carol Fox collected 51 of their original and invented oral stories, told at other times, containing some 43,000 words. She found that many of the spoken stories, as well as revealing a high level of syntactical complexity, were replete with narrative conventions and literary devices, even though the children were very young. For example, in their stories, the children fictionalize themselves, suggest but withhold the secrets of the text (literary theorists will recognise the hermeneutic code!) or use the device of intertextuality, yet all is 'summoned up on the spur of the moment, with no more than seconds for reflection and no time at all for any kind of rehearsal' (Fox, 1988). What particularly interests Carol Fox is how these children, so young, are already using these conventions and devices to explore their own affective domains, but however one looks at it, it is a formidable achievement, affective, literary and linguistic. In their oral stories the children constantly use language like

'And then they were lost indeed till they saw the prettiest house they had never seen ...'

'What was his dismay when they got up there? There was gnashing of teeth ...' (Josh, age 5)

This research shows the forms and functions of written language embedded in the children's spoken language, and both of these in their socio-cultural experience. *Written language is not decontextualized here.* Moreover, as Dr Fox points out, it is very much more sophisticated and advanced than the language of the specially contrived reading schemes that many of these children will meet on entry into school.

Now it is interesting that very little of this kind of research is ever referred to by the people who think that speaking is natural and writing artificial, even to refute it. And even when they do, they usually say that it only applies to *some* children, not all; for example, that it applies to intelligent children, or to middle class children (not true, as the research repeatedly shows). 'It is fully accepted that there are children who learn to read by osmosis ... but you would need a great deal of courage to assume that all children learn in this way ...' (Root, 1986), etc. In particular it is commonly said that learning like this does not apply to children who are having difficulty with reading and writing (as if the immutable processes involved could be changed just for them). My view is that it particularly applies to children with difficulties, and to disadvantaged and inexperienced children, and the evidence shows this.

2   Why are these views, about written language being learnt differently, still believed, in the face of all the evidence?

These views still persist, in my opinion, because for some decades literacy has been misunderstood, and this misunderstanding has become a traditional orthodoxy. For historical reasons I cannot explore now, literacy learning, unlike spoken language learning, has been seen as *linear and hierarchical*. You have to be taught it step by step.

For example, first you have to be taught letters, or sounds, or pictograms, then blending, or letter patterns, or spelling patterns; or first you have to learn one word, then some words; or first you have to learn short words, then longer ones, then even longer ones, then unknown ones, then word attack skills; or first you have to learn to decode or decipher, or to use your phonological knowledge, or your metacognitive knowledge, and then to combine words or to comprehend, and so on, and so on, and so on. The linear model causes a false breakdown into assumed hierarchical skills. This is why learning to read and write is hard work! Like this it is. In fact, considering all the language learning most children have achieved as they learn to speak, learning written language ought to be really easy, not hard at all.

This linear model of literacy learning is still commonly believed and widely practised, and books incorporating it are published all the time. One I came across not long ago is called *Becoming a skilled reader* (already the title is significant). Chapter 4 of the book is called 'Learning to read words' and it says:

'the ability to read words is a *prerequisite* for understanding stories.'
(Oakhill & Garnham, 1988)

The word 'prerequisite' is emphasised in the original. This is not a chance quotation, but the basis of a whole argument. (A similar argument appears in Donaldson's work.)

In fact it is not possible to *read* words, for words *per se* have little or no meaning (Mittins, 1988). You could doubtless decode them to sound, but this has nothing to do with reading. You have to read *much more than words* if you want actually to read (cf. Weaver, 1980). So-called 'word reading' is not reading, nor is it a 'stage' of reading, nor does it lead to reading. Or to put it as Freire does 'You can't read the word without reading the world' (Freire & Macedo, 1987). If Oakhill & Garnham had reversed their statement it would have been much nearer the truth:

'The ability to understand stories is a *prerequisite* for reading words.'

Unfortunately reading is not commonly thought of as total behaviour like this, and many people are so influenced by the traditional skill-based orthodoxy that they cannot conceive of any other possibility. It has become so entrenched that, as Holdaway (1979) says, the very idea that reading and writing might be learned like spoken language gives them a sense of insecurity. 'It is almost as if this type of learning, so manifestly efficient, threatens their professional functions'.

Thus while Donaldson conjectures that in some unspecified way children 'latch on' to spoken language, when it comes to written language they need 'systematic instruction'. Both these words imply a linear model, as incorporated in her reading and language programme *R & D*. This claims to be 'structured', 'graded' and 'sequential' (Reid & Donaldson, 1983). 'Systematic instruction' has nothing to do with real teaching. If you do these things to learners you kill their learning. You take it over and try to do it for them. Children are not automata or parrots. I cannot think of any higher order learning that could be accomplished by 'systematic instruction'.

Perhaps I should just add that from this linear view of literacy learning comes the notion (fairly obviously) that *early* literacy learning is different from *later* literacy learning. In fact children set out to learn everything at once right from the start. A linear or hierarchical model just won't do for what learners do. Harste et al (1984) found that the strategies young 3–6 year old writers followed were of the same order, of the same kind, as mature adult writers. All the research bears this out.

Learning written language, reading or writing, is extremely complex but fairly easy for those involved in the real action, in real reading and real writing as part of real living. For me literacy learning, like spoken language learning and much else, is *cumulative and recursive* – it starts like it ends, though it never ends. I'll stick with Vygotsky:

'In the same way as children learn to speak, they should be able to learn to read and write. Natural methods of teaching reading and writing involve appropriate operations on the child's environment.' (1935, in Vygotsky 1978)

And with my old tutor Nancy Martin. She's 80 now, and after a lifetime of educational experience she writes:

'The way children learn their mother tongue is a potential model for all learning.' (Martin, 1988)

I have pleasure in proposing the motion.

Note

Some of the material is this chapter is included in Hynds, J. (1990) *Real reading* (Tadpole Books Ltd).

References

Bissex, G. (1980) *GNYS AT WRK*. Harvard University Press.
—— (1984) The child as teacher. In Goelman et al (op cit).
Bruner, J. (1984) Language, mind and reading. In Goelman et al (op cit).
Butler, D. (1979) *Cushla and her books*. London: Hodder & Stoughton.
Calkins, L. M. (1980) When children want to punctuate: basic skills belong in context. *Language Arts* 57, 5 May 1980.

—— (1983) *Lessons from a child*. London: Heinemann Educational.

Cazden, C. B., Cordeiro, P. & Giacobbe, M. E. (1985) 'Spontaneous and scientific concepts: young children's learning of punctuation'. In Wells and Nicholls (op cit).

Chafe, W. L. (1985) Linguistic differences produced by differences between speaking and writing. In Olson et al (op cit).

Clark, M. M. (1976) *Young fluent readers*. London: Heinemann Educational.

Clark, M. M. (ed) (1985) *New directions in the study of reading*. Falmer Press.

Cochran-Smith, M. (1984) *The making of a reader*. Norwood, NJ: Ablex Publishing Corporation.

Curtiss, S. (1977) *Genie: a psycholinguistic study of a modern-day 'wild child'*. Academic Press.

Dombey, H. (1983) Learning the language of books. In Meek (1983) (op cit).

—— (1988a) Partners in the telling. In Meek & Mills (op cit).

—— (1988b) Stories at home and at school. In Lightfoot & Martin (op cit).

Donaldson, M. (1984) Speech and writing and modes of learning. In Goelman et al (op cit).

—— (1989) *Sense and sensibility: some thoughts on the teaching of literacy*. Reading: University of Reading.

Donaldson, M. & Reid, J. (1985) Language skills and reading: a developmental perspective. In Clark (op cit).

Ferreiro, E. (1984) The underlying logic of literacy development. In Goelman et al (op cit).

—— (1985) The relationship between oral and written language: the children's viewpoints. In Clark (op cit).

Ferreiro, E. & Teberosky, A. (1983) *Literacy before schooling*. London: Heinemann Educational.

Fox, C. (1983) Talking like a book: young children's oral monologues. In Meek (op cit).

—— (1986) Learning from children learning from home. In *Language Matters* 2 (1986).

—— (1988) Poppies will make them grant. In Meek & Mills (op cit).

—— (1989) Children thinking through story. In *English in Education* 23.2 Summer (1989).

Freire, P. & Macedo, D. (1987) *Literacy: reading the word and the world*. London: Routledge & Kegan Paul.

Fry, D. (1985) *Children talk about books: seeing themselves as readers*. Milton Keynes: Open University Press.

Goelman, H., Oberg, A. & Smith, F. (eds) (1984) *Awakening to literacy*. London: Heinemann Educational.

Hall, N. (1987) *The emergence of literacy.* Edward Arnold/UKRA.

Harste, J. C., Woodward, V. A. & Burke, C. L. (1984) *Language stories and literacy lessons*. London: Heinemann Educational.

Heath, S. B. (1982) What no bedtime story means: narrative skills at home and school. *Language in Society* (11) 49–76.

—— (1983) *Ways with words*. Cambridge: Cambridge University Press.

Hildyard, A. & Hidi, S. (1985) Oral-written differences in the production and recall of narratives. In Olson et al (op cit).

Holdaway, D. (1979) *The foundations of literacy*. Ashton Scholastic.

Ingham, J. (1982) *Books and reading development* (2nd ed). London: Heinemann Educational.

Labov, W. (1969) The logic of nonstandard English, reprinted in Giglioli, P. P. (ed) *Language and social context*. London: Penguin.

Lightfoot, M. & Martin, N. (eds) (1988) *The word for teaching is learning: essays for James Britton*. London: Heinemann Educational.

Martin, M. (1988) Introduction to Lightfoot and Martin (op cit).

Meek, M. (ed) (1983) *Opening moves*. London: University of London.

Meek, M. & Mills, C. (eds) (1988) *Language and learning in the primary school*. Falmer Press.

Mittins, B. (1988) *English: not the naming of parts*. National Association for the Teaching of English.

Moon, C. (1985) *Practical ways to teach reading*. Ward Lock Educational.

Newman, J. (1984) *The craft of children's writing*. London: Scholastic Publications.

Newman, J. (ed) (1985) *Whole language: theory in use*. London: Heinemann Educational.

Oakhill, J. & Garnham, A. (1988) *Becoming a skilled reader*. Oxford: Basil Blackwell.

Olson, D. R. (1977) From utterance to text: the bias of language in speech and writing. *Harvard Educational Review* (47) 3 August 1977.

—— (1984) "See! Jumping!" Some oral antecedents of literacy. In Goelman et al (op cit).

Olson, D. R., Torrance, N. and Hildyard, A. (eds) (1985) *Literacy, language, and learning: the nature and consequences of reading and writing*. Cambridge: Cambridge University Press.

Payton, S. (1984) *Developing awareness of print: a young child's first steps towards literacy*. Birmingham: University of Birmingham.

Perera, K. (1984) *Children's reading and writing*. Oxford: Basil Blackwell.

—— (1986) Grammatical differentiation between speech and writing by children aged 8 to 12. In Wilkinson, A. (ed) *The writing of writing*. Milton Keynes: Open University Press.

—— (1987) *Understanding language*. National Association of Advisers in English.

Read, C. (1986) *Children's creative spelling*. London: Routledge & Kegan Paul.

Reid, J. & Donaldson, M. (1983) *R & D: An integrated reading and language programme for the primary years*. London: Macmillan.

Root, B. (1986) *In defence of reading schemes*. Reading: University of Reading.

Rosen, M. (1989) *Did I hear you write?* London: Andre Deutsch.

Sapir, E. (1921) *Language: an introduction to the study of speech*. Harcourt, Brace & World.

Smith, F. (1983) Demonstrations, engagement and sensitivity . In *Essays into literacy*. London: Heinemann Educational.

Stainthorp, R. (1989) 'A balanced approach to the teaching of literacy'. In *Reading* (23) 2 July 1989.

Street, B. V. (1984) *Literacy in theory and practice*. Cambridge: Cambridge University Press.

Stubbs, M. (1980) *Language and literacy: the sociolinguistics of reading and writing*. London: Routledge & Kegan Paul.

Taylor, D. (1983) *Family literacy: young children learning to read and write*. London: Heinemann Educational.

Temple, C., Nathan, R., Burris, N. & Temple, F. (1988) *The beginnings of writing* (2nd ed). Allyn and Bacon.

Torrance, N. & Olson, D. R. (1985) Oral and literate competencies in the early school years . In Olson et al (op cit).

Vygotsky, L. S. (1978) *Mind in society: the development of higher psychological processes*. Harvard University Press.

Weaver, C. (1980) Why is a word-identification view of reading inappropriate? Chapter 5 of *Psycholinguistics and reading: from process to practice*. Little, Brown & Company.

Wells, G. (1985a) 'Pre-school literacy related activities and success in school'. In Olson et al (op cit).

—— (1985b) Language and learning: an interactional perspective. In Wells and Nicholls (op cit).

—— (1986) *The meaning makers: children learning language and using language to learn*. London: Hodder & Stoughton.

Wells, G. & Nicholls, J. (eds) (1985) *Language and learning: an interactional perspective*. Falmer Press.

9 We learn written language much as we learn spoken language... (against)

John Bald

Jeff Hynds has argued that, although spoken language and written language are different, they are learned in the same way. He has even come close to arguing that *everything* is learned in the same way. He also stated that 'reading words has nothing to do with reading'. These statements are, I believe, important errors. They are at the crux of this debate and together constitute a fundamental and fatal flaw in his argument.

Research by Marie Clay and Katharine Perera has shown a strong relationship both between the ability to recognise words quickly, and the qualities of phrasing and intonation which make reading come alive. Katharine Perera's research (presented at the 1988 UK Reading Association Conference, but not yet in print), involved taping children reading at three-monthly intervals between the ages of six and eight. The samples were transcribed above a three-line musical stave, which allowed her to assess pitch and phrasing as well as accuracy, and she found that it was not until children were reading at speeds of 60–70 words per minute that they began to group words together instead of 'barking at print'. In Marie Clay's observation of 100 young readers in Auckland, she found that the highest quartile of a sample of six-year-olds were both reading much more than the lowest quartile, were reading much more accurately and were reading much faster. Their error rate was one word in 37 compared with one in three for the weakest quartile, their error correction rate was one in three compared to one in 210, their mean speed was 1.02 seconds per word compared to 1.57 seconds per word and they read roughly seven times as many words during the observations.

No one is going to argue that word recognition is all there is to

reading – we know, for example, that children use their knowledge of grammatical forms in making sense of sentences – but
both of these pieces of research show that if you can't recognise
words you can't read. The fact is recognised implicitly in miscue
analysis, where 95 per cent or so of words must be recognised on
sight before it can work, and accounts for the high correlations
between word recognition tests and more sophisticated reading
assessments. It is also behind Vygotsky's analysis of the different
patterns in learning spoken language and writing in *Thought and
Language*:[1]

'Written speech is a separate linguistic function, differing from oral
speech in both structure and mode of functioning. Even its minimal
development requires a high level of abstraction. It is speech in thought
and mind only, lacking the musical, expressive, intonational qualities of
oral speech. In learning to write, the child must disengage himself from
the sensory aspect of speech and replace words by images of words.
Speech that is merely imagined and that requires symbolization of the
sound image in written signs (ie a secondary degree of symbolization)
naturally must be much harder than oral speech for the child as algebra
is harder than arithmetic. Our studies show that it is the abstract quality
of written language that is the main stumbling block ...'

Jeff Hynds recognises, like Vygotsky, the differences between
speech and writing, but chooses to ignore the consequences of
these differences for learning. When Vygotsky argued that it
would eventually be possible for children to learn written language
'naturally', he was developing an approach from Montessori's
work on building bridges between the child and the abstract world
of print. He does not suggest a simple transfer of learning
strategies from spoken language to print.

Vygotsky, however, has more to say about writing than reading, and this debate concerns both. At the last UKRA debate, I
opposed Dr Joyce Morris's motion that 'phonics are essential to
learning to read', partly on the grounds that some children could
not handle the abstract reasoning required by the phonics. Since
then, the long-term results of Dr Lynnette Bradley's research[2]
have appeared, showing that specific training in the categorisation
of sound patterns, followed by the relation of the sounds to letters,
can make a great difference to both spelling and writing to children whose initial perception of these patterns was weak. After 40
ten-minute training sessions, spread over two years, a group which

had received this type of extra teaching had made progress against three control groups in both reading and spelling and the differences were still statistically significant over four years after the project had ended. If written language and spoken language were learned in the same way, this highly structured teaching would not have made so much difference.

The one case I know of where children with difficulties were taught in a way that did not require them to pay conscious attention to detail produced a much less happy outcome. Margaret Meek's *Achieving literacy*,[3] in which a group of teachers spent several hours per week individually trying to help weak readers in a secondary school without drawing their attention to individual words, produced no evidence of progress whatsoever. The author is frank enough to admit this, but the agonising of the teachers as they try to cope with the pupils' realisation that the method is not working is both painful and unnecessary. A personal visit from Frank Smith, who endorsed the approach, seems to have carried much more weight in their thinking than the reality of their pupils' problems. The lowest ebb is on page 216, where one pupil explains to his teacher that he is going to truant from his examinations, because he can't read the papers. The dialogue is as follows:

Teacher: ... I try again and say 'These exams are five weeks away. Anything can happen in five weeks.'

Then Trevor: 'Oh yes miss, who are you kidding? I've been coming for three and a half years with you ... I'm not going to learn to read in five weeks.'

The one question to which Trevor lacks an answer is why the teacher has such faith in what she is doing. I share his bewilderment. Not one of the the vast list of references Jeff Hynds has offered as 'evidence' in this debate shows any better outcome from the use of this wholistic approach with failing readers. I suggest that the reason he uses so many references is that it avoids the problem of selecting specific evidence to support his case.

My final point does not concern children with problems, but Art, in the form of Jill Pirrie's approach to teaching poetry in her book *On common ground*.[4] Jeff joins me in praising this book, but does not appreciate the extent to which it damages his case. Poetry, for Jill Pirrie, is based on personal experience and memory, but is the result of intensive reflection on that experience, which is re-worked and condensed to form what she describes as language in its most concentrated form. Spoken language has a role in its production, but the whole process is so far removed from everyday speech as to constitute a highly specific activity which stretches the linguistic, intellectual and emotional resources of the child to the limit. The essence of Jill Pirrie's achievement is to make this artistic experience available to children of a broad range of ability in school, and its extent can only be understood by reading the children's work and considering in detail the learning processes which she has set up. There could be no better demonstration of the fact that we do not learn everything in the same way, or that some types of learning require much more intensive attention to detail than others.

The remaining question in terms of this debate is how the idea contained in the motion has come to enjoy its present level of support and acceptance. The answer is, I think, twofold. In the first place, it is partly true for all children, and apparently wholly true for others, who learn to read at such an early age that the process appears to be spontaneous. The second reason is that the idea allows us to go straight from the child to the areas of experience and development which have invariably influenced our own experience of literature and which are at the core of our civilised values. Our perspective as literate people enables us to make such a leap, and we have all seen children make it too. Unfortunately, the school of reading development dominated by Frank Smith and Kenneth Goodman, and represented by Jeff Hynds, insists on such cases as the whole truth and ignores or dismisses with a joke the more complex and detailed learning processes which many children have to go through in the process of becoming literate. The motion is a half-truth and should be rejected.

Notes

1 Vygotsky, L. S. *Thought and language*: MIT Press, 1962.
2 Bald, J. Connecting patterns. *The Times Educational Supplement*, 18.3.88.
3 Meek, M. et al *Achieving literacy*. RKP, 1983.
4 Pirrie, J. *On common ground*. London: Hodder & Stoughton, 1987.

10 My problems with real reading

Geoffrey Lewis

I am worried about the nature of some of the arguments which are
deployed in support of the 'real books' approach to the learning of
reading. It is not that I feel the approach to be 'wrong'; on the
contrary I believe it makes a powerful and unique contribution to
the understanding of how young children learn to read. However,
I do feel that the argumentation sometimes lacks rigour and sometimes fails to analyse important aspects of process.

On the topic of change in classroom practice, Waterland (1988)
states:

'Classroom practice should always have a firm and respectable intellectual basis. We cannot any longer – if we ever really could – offer only
feelings or instincts as our rationale. This is especially true if we are
changing established practice. What will be our justification? Is what we
are planning better only in our opinion or can we find support from
outside authorities? Any change should deepen and enlarge our understanding of children, reading and teaching.' (p 10)

Change can be evolutionary or revolutionary. Proponents of
revolution sometimes find themselves handling discussion in ways
which are misleading and logically inadequate. Within the 'real
books' debate, the points I would like to take up are:

1   The adoption of an adversarial stance.
2   Economy of truth.
3   The misrepresentation of others' viewpoints.
4   The failure to acknowledge the interpretative nature of evi-
    dence.
5   The failure fully to analyse the processes which are invoked in
    support of the argument.

The adversarial stance is reflected in comments which denigrate
the 'other' approaches to the teaching of reading, eg

'These, then, are the ideas which challenge most of the conventional practices in our schools; reading schemes, vocabulary control, colour coding, phonic drill, reading tests – all are concentrating on the wrong things. They are obsessed with teaching decoding, not with helping children to become readers.' (Waterland, 1988, p 19)

Even if the final sentence is true, this stance only encourages opinion to harden one way or another. In an effort to convince, it is possible to lapse into economy of truth, as in this discussion of 'traditional' methods:

'This is, broadly, the way thousands of children learn to read, and by its own criteria, it is often successful. Many children do progress from skill to skill fairly satisfactorily and return average scores on reading tests.' (Waterland, 1988, p 11)

Is the claim really that such children never attain scores *above* average? Or that the approach is only satisfactory by its own criteria and no others?

One consequence of this adversarial position is that the accumulated insights and research evidence stemming from other approaches is disregarded or even denied. It is possible to dispute some of this evidence on the grounds of faulty design or the making of unwarranted assumptions; however, to dismiss it out of hand is manifestly unprofessional, and a very great setback to the development of a comprehensive theory of reading.

In any case the argument only appears clear-cut and reasonable because of the misrepresentation of 'other' viewpoints. What often seems to happen is that an opposing viewpoint is created, rather than referred to. For example,

'Before this particular linguistic revolution made any impact on education, reading was thought of as a discrete and separate skill, or perhaps a bundle of special skills. Learning to read was a decoding task ...' (Whitehead, 1987, p 21)

'Reading was viewed as a hierarchy of specific skills, a taxonomy of behaviours, which, if taught in small enough units, one upon the other, with rewards for each demonstration of success, could be built up into a total edifice of reading ability.' (Waterland, 1988, p 8)

'To concentrate on the technicalities of decoding, whether by flashcards or phonic games is to remove reading from the business of making sense of the world and to turn it into the production of a set of empty mechanical responses to the teacher's demands.' (Dombey, 1987, p 17)

'The traditional approach to learning to read takes the view that reading essentially consists of a hierarchy of skills to be mastered in small steps, one at a time in sequence and gradually built up into a whole.' (Bennet, 1988, p 17)

These summaries are not claimed to represent any specific work or author. They suggest a uniformity of 'traditional practice' which fails to appreciate the actual diversity of existing practice. The summaries are therefore an interpretation, weakened by the fact that no source is quoted. In fact, some of the most obvious targets, the reading scheme manuals, would deny some or all of the criticisms. For example:

'The child learns by the repetition but does not lose interest in the context.' (Munro, 1954, p 27)

'The ideas can be grouped around three main principles. These are:
1   That a reading programme must aim to make learning as **simple, natural and meaningful** as possible for all children, and must not sacrifice one of these qualities to another.
2   That children's learning must be fostered and structured by **linking** new experiences to what is already known, and by linking one area of knowledge to another.
3   That learning to read and write must be viewed as **kinds of language learning.**'

(Reid and Low, 1973, p 10)

The situation is clearly not as simple as has been suggested, and the rather emotive tones of the real reading advocates seem unjustified. I would suggest that the quotations from the manuals show that the approaches are better seen as complementary rather than oppositional in nature.

It is a distinct barrier to progress if a particular approach seeks only to support its own contentions. Any position becomes infinitely more reliable if it sets out to **disconfirm** its own beliefs and assumptions. If contrary evidence is not actively sought, then at least it is necessary to consider alternative interpretations of the data. One pitfall is to accept one's own understanding as 'true', and not appreciate that evidence can usually be construed in more than one way. For example, Dombey's claim that, 'To concentrate on the technicalities of decoding ... is to remove reading from the business of making sense of the world and to turn it into the production of a set of empty mechanical responses ...' **may** be true **in some instances**. It is also likely to be wrong in some cases;

if learning to read includes some growing perception of the nature of language, then certain word analysis activities removed from the context of a 'real text' may be very meaningful for a particular reader. It all depends on the reader's understanding and purpose, and the ways in which they interact with those of the teacher. Children not only enjoy stories (whatever that may mean), they also enjoy a sense of growing mastery in a purposeful area. 'Making sense of the world' may well include growing appreciation of the nature of the language we use, and an increasing ability to make use of that knowledge in independent reading. It is paradoxical that those who stress the uniqueness of the reader's response to text often deny such differentiation in other areas of process.

The 'real reading' analysis is a persuasive account of the circumstances in which many children acquire the ability to read effectively and with enjoyment. However to set this up as a comprehensive programme for literacy acquisition we need more information. To be effective we need to know such things as

a   The conditions associated with successful learning.
b   The processes which occur during reading.
c   The effect of the text on these processes.

The 'real books' approach has a valuable contribution to make in these areas. However, this has not been maximally achieved because many of its advocates have stopped short after considering the first, and have not addressed the other two issues. Indeed, there seems to be a view that any analysis of process in terms of components is somehow undesirable or wrong. 'Reading is not a series of small skills fluently used; it is a process of getting meaning' (Waterland, 1988, p 14). To support this, we need to know what is meant by getting meaning, and something of the process involved. We need this information in order to model this process for the reader, frame appropriate questions, vary the activities to optimise the effect, and so on. In the first place we need to query whether reading is best defined as a process of *getting* meaning. That wording suggests that meaning is some sort of product, the target of reading. However according to some models of reading (including that implicitly espoused by Waterland), on-going meaning is also used in a predictive manner, with implications for the amount of perceptual processing required. Reading is more than getting meaning; it is a matter of *using* meaning. Two implications arise.

Firstly, we need to define what we mean by meaning. This is an issue relating to the representation of knowledge and as such lies within the province of cognitive psychology. In the same way, the process of getting meaning must be analysed, unless we assume that this process is in some way indivisible. In fact, current work on models of reading (eg de Beaugrande, 1981) includes many insights which are very compatible with the view that reading cannot easily be split into sub-skills operating sequentially. Reading may, in fact, comprise sub-skills, but working simultaneously and in interactive fashion. If this is so, it is predictable that many problems of those learning to read will concern the integration of skills, and the management of unconscious processes. The paired reading approach, reflecting as it does an inductive approach to learning, is particularly suited to this type of problem. What is needed is an inter-disciplinary approach, in which each discipline illumines the others, rather than scores points at others' expense.

Secondly, it is clear that text plays an important part in the creation of meaning. We need to look beyond the dimensions of naturalness or interest. For example, what is it in the selection and ordering of text items which helps to create certain types of understanding, or even the interest which is so highly valued? What is the effect of varying and manipulating text form, and how can this be used to benefit readers? It seems odd that an approach which stresses the importance of the provision of effective texts should pay so little attention to the clarification of what it is that makes any particular text so effective, or to the development of criteria which would enable teachers to communicate about why a text is so good/bad. Yet the links are there to be made; there are several forms of text analysis which offer more than a set of descriptive categories and which illumine the way(s) in which a text creates communication. Take as an example the issue of text type. Texts which are designed to provide information have a different structure from those which are designed to entertain as stories. Well-written expository texts are clear, unambiguous and to the point. In contrast, stories are often written to be ambiguous, misleading and non-obvious (see de Beaugrande, 1980, for a discussion of this aspect of storiness). Non-fiction texts on familiar topics may in some ways be more 'readable' than stories.

The apparent preference for stories interacts with the assumption that valid texts must necessarily be complex. Whitehead (1987) says that:

'... the approach depends on the use of complex human texts as reading material. Complex human texts embody recognisable issues, motives and emotions in recognisable language. In other words, stories, anecdotes and real books are the ideal narrative texts for beginning readers.' (p 21)

There are two issues I would like to discuss arising from this statement; these relate to the matter of text type, and to the role of complexity.

Since text serves to communicate, there is no reason why we should be limited to one function, that of telling stories. The devaluing of non-fiction texts is worrying. They become increasingly important as vehicles of learning and personal development, yet are often given less attention than literary texts. *English for ages 5 to 16* (DES, 1989) has a whole chapter on literary texts. Expository texts are given much less attention and tend to be seen as providers of material for 'information retrieval', which does not do justice to the excitement of ideas experienced by some readers of non-fiction texts. Such excitement is surely as important as an equivalent response to stories. It should be remembered that non-fiction texts are preferred reading for some. The Assessment of Performance Unit's analysis of attitudes to reading (APU, 1981) found that 30 per cent of children responding to the stem, 'The thing I like best about reading is ...', talked in terms of self-improvement. Particular reference was made to the acquisition of further knowledge.

The issue of complexity touches upon many of the assumptions underlying the 'real books' approach. The belief that to analyse complexity in some way does damage to the object of our interest limits drastically any attempt to explore the reading process so that we may teach more effectively and with greater insight. I believe a more rewarding approach to be that suggested by Minsky (1987):

'What makes a drawing more than just its separate lines?
How is a personality more than a set of traits?
In what ways is a culture more than a mere collection of customs?

What makes a tower more than separate blocks?
Why is a chain more than its various links?
How is a wall more than a set of many bricks?

Why do the 'objective' questions seem less mysterious? Because we have good ways to answer them – in terms of how things interact. 'Subjective' reactions are also based on how things interact. The difference is that here we are not concerned with objects in the world outside, but with processes inside our brains.'

If complexity is seen in terms of as yet unexplained interactions it sets up a very exciting prospect in which individual teachers' observations of individual readers may genuinely further our understanding of the reading process.

Another tenet of the 'real books' argument which warrants exploration is the relationship between learning to read and learning to speak. By some, the two processes are seen as almost identical. Waterland does say that 'This is not to claim that what goes on in the child's head is the same for both skills' (p 13). However we need to go beyond undeveloped ideas of immersion, and use insights relating to language acquisition in a systematic way. The context in which children learn to speak is one in which they may adopt an inductive learning style in which they generate and test hypotheses about the nature and structure of language. Among the factors which seem to facilitate learning are:

- Considerable repetition of certain lexical, syntactic and pragmatic features;
- Considerable contextual support;
- The production of 'simple' forms by the conversational partner (although this is not observed in all societies (see Heath, 1983);
- The tailoring of utterances to suit individual need and level – many conversational exchanges involve few turns (in contrast to many written texts).

Some of these features are very reminiscent of those espoused by the maligned reading schemes. Closer examination of what is known about spoken language acquisition may, in fact, reconcile the 'real books' approach with that which advocates a more structured approach to the teaching of reading. It is also possible to identify ways in which the two processes differ and which must have implications for process. In particular there is the imposition of a level of language processing with a complex state of relationships between visual, phonological and morphemic aspects of language.

Another aspect of the learning to read process which merits attention is the developmental dimension. It is correctly pointed out that children learn to speak without explicit, formal teaching. Some may learn to read in a similar way. That does not mean that there is no other way. Children make very effective use of the inductive learning mode when learning to speak. However, as they grow older, they become increasingly able to learn in a deductive manner. Learning can be increasingly focused and made more effective. The question is not about which is the best/only way, but about a child's learning status on both these styles of learning, so that the two learning modes can be most effectively combined.

In conclusion, there is no doubt that the 'real books' approach to reading has much to offer, including some unique advantages over other techniques. However, it cannot provide a complete account of factors involved in learning to read, and therefore its proponents now need to look beyond the literary domain and seek a synthesis of ideas and concepts from disparate disciplines, particularly text and discourse analysis, cognitive psychology and artificial intelligence. The combination, not only of information, but also of ways of thinking and of seeking evidence will be of value to all.

References

Assessment of Performance Unit (1981) *Language performance in schools. Primary survey report No. 1*. London: HMSO.

de Beaugrande, R. (1980) *Text, discourse and process*. London: Longman.

—— (1981) Design criteria for process models of reading. In *Reading Research Quarterly*, vol 16, no 2, pp 261–315.

Bennet, J. (1988) Reading, but what? In *Books For Your Children* vol 23, no 3, pp 17–18.

DES (1989) *English for ages 5 to 16*. London: HMSO.

Dombey, H. (1987) Reading for real from the start. In *English In Education* vol 21, no 2, pp 12–19.

Heath, S. B. (1983) *Ways with words*. Cambridge: Cambridge University Press.

Minsky, M. (1987) *The society of mind*. London: Heinemann.

Munro, J. (1954) *Janet and John: Teachers' Manual*. London: Nisbet.

Reid, J. F. and Low, J. (1973) *The written word*. (Link-Up Manual). Edinburgh: Holmes-McDougall.

Waterland, L. (1988) *Read with me* (2nd edition). Stroud: Thimble Press.

Whitehead, M. (1987) Reading – caught or taught? Some issues involved in the changed approaches to the teaching of reading. In *English In Education* vol 21, no 2, pp 20–25.

11 Literacy learning in a multiethnic primary classroom: an ethnographic study

Rebecca Huss

This past decade has seen a virtual explosion of research into early literacy acquisition. Research has been focused on beginning literacy learning within the classroom (Dyson, 1983, 1985, 1986; Cochran-Smith, 1984), on what young children know about print (Ferreiro and Teberosky, 1982; Harste, Woodward and Burke, 1984; Blazer, 1986; Rabin, 1986), on how the home environment can be conducive to literacy learning (Clark, 1976; Taylor, 1983; Gundlach et al, 1985; Taylor and Dorsey-Gaines, 1988), and how the children's cultural context influences literacy learning (Heath, 1983; Schieffelin and Cochran-Smith, 1984).

Virtually all this research, however, has focused on young children's literacy learning in their mother tongue, usually English. As Great Britain becomes more ethnically and linguistically diverse, it becomes increasingly important that educators and researchers focus as well on what factors help contribute to successful beginning literacy learning for children whose mother tongue is not English.

Success in English literacy is often the springboard for success in school, and society in general, for second language learners (Wallace, 1988). Despite the importance of this issue, little research has been done in Great Britain to examine just what factors contribute to success in beginning second language literacy learning (Atkinson, Delamond, Hammersley, 1988).

During the 1988–89 academic year, I undertook an ethnographic study of beginning literacy learning in a class of 5–6 year old children in a multiethnic primary school in an urban area in the north of England. I sought to discover the ways in which young children successfully begin the literacy learning process in a second language.

From within the class, I selected eight case study children, six of whom were second language learners, who demonstrated a range of literacy learning styles and abilities. The children included four Punjabi speaking Pakistani girls, a Punjabi speaking Pakistani boy and a Somali Language speaking boy. Their language proficiency ranged from beginning level to almost fluent level English. The children were from mainly working class families and they ranged in age from 5.8 to 6.2 years old when the main data collection began in January 1989.

I used a variety of techniques for gathering data on children's reading, writing and oral language both inside and outside the classroom. My role within the classroom was as a participant observer; the children viewed me as a teacher assistant. Three to four days a week from January to June I took field notes of literacy activities within the classroom, assisted at the writing table with spelling, and dictation of story (the class used a copy writing rather than a developmental writing approach). I audiotaped talk around the writing table and collected samples of children's written work. Additionally, I read with the children, I interviewed the children, teachers and administrators, as well as the children's parents within the homes using translators. I attended Koranic class at Mosque School and visited classrooms both within the school and outside the school for comparison purposes. My goal was to get as broad a picture as possible of the children's literacy learning.

This chapter, then, will outline some of the factors that my data analysis revealed that help to contribute to these particular children's successful second language literacy learning. Because this is an ethnographic study, no attempt is being made to generalise the findings to all second language learners or even to all Punjabi or Somali language speakers. However, it is hoped that insights gained from this study of these children's attempts at beginning literacy learning will aid educators and researchers in examining similar factors in other second language learners, and thereby contributing to a greater understanding of beginning second language literacy learning.

Factors contributing to successful second language literacy learning

Based on interviews with children and their parents as well as observations within the class, I have found several factors which are present with children who are successful second language literacy learners.

1   *Children see a future-oriented reason for literacy learning*

When asked 'Why are you learning to read and write?', they gave answers which were oriented to the future:

'If anybody asks you then you'll know.'
'You will know books when you're big. You'll know everything. You'll learn.'
'So you can read books at home.'
'When you get to a bigger class, then you'll know.'
'Because when you go to big school you'll know how to write.'

These children can see a purpose for reading and writing. In contrast, some children had no idea why they were being taught to read and write.

The children who saw a future-oriented purpose for reading and writing had older siblings or relatives who interacted with them with literacy. They knew about 'the bigger class' and the type of work that is done there, as well as why it is important to be a good reader and writer for later success. In other words, they had positive role models.

2   *The children were active, risk-taking literacy learners who showed an avid interest in literacy learning*

Because the children saw a reason for reading and writing, they then actively pursued their goal of becoming literate. In doing so, the successful literacy learners took risks. They attempted to spell words on their own, to read books on their own and to figure out words using independent strategies such as a combination of picture, context and phonics clues rather than being constantly dependent on the teacher to tell them the words. Harste, Woodward and Burke note that, 'it is via the process of risk-taking that language learning and, hence, growth in literacy occurs' (1984, p 136). By not being afraid to make a mistake this growth could then take place.

When the children did need help in reading or writing, such as how a word is spelled, what a word means, how something is drawn, they actively sought help from both peers and adults. The children were characterised by their parents as children who asked a lot of questions and who were very curious about the world around them.

This curiosity and reaching out to others permeated their talk at the writing table with both teachers and peers. They asked others questions, commented on their own and others' work, among other kinds of talk. Talk helped these children to formulate and develop their story ideas in English.

Additionally, these children actively practised literacy at home. They looked at and read books, wrote and drew at home.

3 The children had family members who were actively involved in the child's literacy learning

So often I heard from educators that there was not much literacy going on in these children's homes, that the mothers were illiterate, that the families did not care about the children's literacy learning, that the parents regarded the home as their responsibility and the school the teacher's responsibility. Based on my interviews with children and parents, I found these assumptions not to be accurate.

Children who had become active, independent risk-taking literacy learners did so not solely on their own, but through the help of adults in their lives, both teachers and family members. These children exemplified Vygotsky's notion that 'what a child can do in cooperation today, he can do alone tomorrow' (1962, p 104).

Parents and other family members were actively involved in literacy learning in each home I visited. In the homes where the mother was not literate in English, someone else filled the role of literacy mentor, an older sister, an aunty, an older cousin. Most often the person that read to the child or to whom the child read was a female. Literacy was definitely a female-oriented activity in these homes. The main role of the males in the family was to take the children to the public library since it was some distance away and necessitated going by car or bus. Almost every successful literacy learner used both the school and public library.

Another important family role was promoting mother tongue and religious literacy learning. The Pakistani children's written script is Urdu and some of the mothers were already beginning to teach their children how to read and write Urdu. One mother showed me the copy book she and her daughter were using where the mother wrote the Urdu alphabet and the daughter copied under it, the same method used at school.

Religious literacy is also important to these families who were all observant Muslims. Parents whose children did not attend nightly Mosque School, spent time with them each evening teaching them the Arabic script of the Kaida, the catechism book of the Koran. Arabic is a script for which they have no spoken equivalent and whose script resembles the Urdu script in appearance and directionality (read right to left, books open back to front).

In the Pakistani children's homes then, they regularly encounter scripts in English, Arabic and Urdu and spoken languages of Punjabi, Urdu and English. In the Somali child's home, he encounters writing in English, Somali language (which shares the same script and directionality as English), as well as Arabic with different script and directionality and spoken languages of English and Somali language. In each case the families serve as literacy mediators for the children.

These children's parents have high aspirations for their children. All of them want their children to go on to higher education if the child is capable and they see English language literacy as a route to this educational goal. Equally, mother tongue literacy and religious literacy are also goals these parents have for their children.

So, children who see a future-oriented reason for learning literacy, who are actively interested in literacy learning, who are willing to take risks and who have active involvement of family members in their literacy learning are those second language learners that are found to be the most successful literacy learners.

Implications for practice

What implications do these findings have for teachers and researchers involved with young second language learners? Several classroom implications can be derived:

1 Teachers need to explore with children just why they are learning to read and write as well as the purposes for reading and writing. This may be obvious to teachers, but it is not always obvious to the children, especially those with limited second language literacy experiences. Second language children often come with the perspective of the ways reading and writing are used in their culture, for religious purposes for example, and may need to be introduced to additional uses of literacy, such as for communication and enjoyment. These uses need to be promoted in the classroom.

2 Teachers need to make sure the classroom is an environment where children feel comfortable and are not afraid to make a mistake or to take risks. This low-risk environment is especially important for second language learners who are often learning both the oral and written forms of English simultaneously.

In order to move the children beyond the strategy of 'ask the teacher' that seemed to be so common, perhaps due to the way they are taught the Kaida at Mosque School, teachers need to give children alternative strategies as to what to do when they do not know something. How can they find out independently or with the help of peers?

Additionally, conversation in small groups around the writing table needs to be encouraged. Talk, especially for second language learners, helps them to formulate their ideas in English and gives them an opportunity to gain feedback and story ideas from teachers and peers. My research showed conversation around the writing table to be a rich source of oral language for young children. Audiotaping and transcribing the conversation at intervals throughout the school year can help teachers monitor growth in second language learning.

3 I found that second language parents *are* interested in their children's learning, but often the language barrier, especially on

the part of the mothers, prevents them from being able to communicate effectively with their children's teachers. Also, the parents often come from educational backgrounds where assumptions about how literacy is taught are very different and where parent involvement is not encouraged in the schools. These factors make it necessary for the teachers and the schools actively to reach out to second language parents rather than automatically expecting the same degree of parent involvement in the schools as with native English speaking parents. I found home visits using a translator known to the parents is a very effective form of communication. This initial investment in time and effort done early in the school year could yield big benefits in informing the parents about how literacy is taught in the school, and encouraging them in their attempts to help their child at home with literacy. A short video could even be made showing excerpts from the school day explained in mother tongue and shared with parents since almost all the homes have a video recorder.

An on-going parent newsletter about what the children are doing in class could be sent home along with easy ways families can help children at home with literacy learning. Ideally these could be in dual language.

Additional classroom ethnographic studies need to be done to explore other aspects of beginning literacy learning with different groups of young second language learners to determine other classroom and cultural factors that contribute to successful second language literacy learning. By continued research translated into effective practice, successful literacy learning can be within the grasp of an ever-increasing number of our young second language learners.

References

Atkinson, P., Delamont, S. & Hammersley, M. (1988) Qualitative research traditions: a British response to Jacob. *Review of Educational Research*, 58 (2), pp 231–250.
Blazer, B. (1986) I want to talk to you about writing: five year old children speak. In Schieffelin, B. & Gilmore, P. (eds), *The acquisition of literacy: ethnographic perspectives* (pp 75–109). Norwood, N.J.: Ablex Publishing.
Clark, M. (1976) *Young fluent readers*. London: Heinemann.

Cochran-Smith, M. (1984) *The making of a reader*. Norwood, N.J.: Ablex Publishing.

Dyson, A. H. (1985) Individual differences in emerging writing. In Farr, M. (ed), *Advances in writing research vol 1: Children's early writing development* (pp 59–125). Norwood, N.J.: Ablex Publishing.

—— (1986) Transitions and tensions: Interrelationships between the drawing, talking and dictating of young children. *Research in the teaching of English*, 20 (4), pp 379–409.

Ferreiro, E. & Teberosky, A. (1982) *Literacy before schooling*. London: Heinemann.

Gundlach, R., McLane, J., Stott, F. & McNamee, G. (1985) Social foundations of children's early writing development. In Farr, M. (ed), *Advances in writing research vol 1: Children's early writing development* (pp 1–58). Norwood, N.J.: Ablex Publishing.

Harste, J., Woodward, V. & Burke, C. (1984) *Language stories and literacy lessons*. London: Heinemann.

Heath, S. B. (1983) *Ways with words*. Cambridge, Mass: Cambridge University Press.

Rabin, B. (1986) *Children's thinking about reading and writing*. Occasional paper no 1. Reading and Language Information Centre, University of Reading, School of Education.

Schieffelin, B. & Cochran-Smith, M. (1984) Learning to read culturally: literacy before schooling. In Goelman, H., Oberg, A. & Smith, F. (eds), *Awakening to literacy* (pp 3–23). London: Heinemann.

Taylor, D. (1983) *Family literacy: young children learning to read and write*. London: Heinemann.

Taylor, D. & Dorsey-Gaines, C. (1988) *Growing up literate*. Portsmouth, N.H.: Heinemann.

Vygotsky, L. S. (1962) *Thought and language*. Cambridge, Mass: Harvard University Press.

Wallace, C. (1988) *Learning to read in a multicultural society: the social context of second language literacy*. London: Prentice Hall.

12 The different registers of texts across the curriculum and what some pupils have to say about them

Alison Littlefair

As pupils progress through school, they endeavour to read books which are written in a variety of registers. 'Register' is a complex linguistic feature which many linguists understand to be closely linked to another linguistic feature, 'genre'.

In this sense genres are seen as the purposeful activities which make up the culture in which we live. We learn to act in ways, or genres, which are meaningful to others. Thus we may talk of the genre of the classroom, the genre of buying and selling, the genre of holidays. In this sense, 'genre' is not simply describing a category of things but rather a way of going about things. This idea of genre has been described by Jim Martin of Sydney University:

'For us, a genre is a staged, goal oriented activity in which speakers engage as members of our culture. Virtually everything you do involves you participating in one or other genre.' (Martin, 1984, p 28)

A genre itself is abstract. Any genre has a purpose and is communicated through language by 'register' patterning. We are never completely free to use language in any way we wish for we are, to some extent, constrained by the situation we find ourselves in. We may wonder how we know what patterning of language or 'register' to use. How do we speak or write and make sense within a situation? In order to do this, we are implicitly aware of the communicative situation we are in. Firstly, we will be concerned with a particular subject or area of interest. Secondly, the situation will necessitate either spoken or written communication between communicator and communicatee who may be face to face as in a conversation or distanced as in a radio broadcast. In addition, there will be some kind of relationship between the communicator and the communicatee which may range from intimate to very formal. Halliday (1985) has respectively termed these aspects of a communicative situation which can be written or spoken: the field, the mode, and the tenor of discourse. We implicitly express the field, mode and tenor of our discourse by using different patterning of vocabulary and grammar. This interaction results in a spoken or written register. Such patterning represents different kinds of meaning within our culture. As teachers, we have the responsibility of enabling children to experience and become familiar with a wide range of both spoken and written registers.

Very young children seem to learn different registers of *spoken* language. Most children know that they do not address their teachers in the same way as they talk to their friends in the play-ground.

I believe that the registers of *written* language are not as success-fully learned since children's experience and use of them is nothing like as extensive. Some children seem to assimilate an awareness of register patterning as they develop as readers, but other children may become more effective readers more quickly if they are helped to be more aware of the meaning of different registers.

Donaldson (1989) urges teachers to help children to look upon language, 'as a flexible system over which they can gradually extend their power' (p 27).

Kress, in Unsworth (1984), has described the aim of reading as providing, 'access for all children to the cultural forms of the society in which they live'. We have, however, paid little attention to the different genres of books which we give to children. We have been aware of the different texts which we associate with different subject areas but we have mainly been concerned with pupils' cognitive understanding of the content. It is, of course, almost impossible to separate the cognitive aspect from the lin-guistic aspect of texts. We should be far more aware of the inter-action of meaning, text and context.

One way of looking at the different genres of books used across the curriculum is to categorise them, on the basis of the different purposes of writers, into four genres: *literary, expository, procedu-*

ral, reference. Each genre is expressed through a different although flexible register patterning.

There has been very little research into how far children are aware of different register patterns. In an attempt to explore this, I asked 72 pupils of different ages and ability to talk about pages taken from different genres of books from across the curriculum. Each pupil discussed with me the similarities and differences between the pages. Their responses indicate something of the varying degrees of awareness and of difficulty which the pupils experienced as they read different register patterns.

Responses to pages from the literary genre

The writer whose purpose is to narrate or describe personal or vicarious experience uses a *literary* genre. Sub-genres could be stories of all kinds, plays, or poetry.

Some third year junior school readers were not always fully aware of the field, or content area of an adventure story:

'I think it's more adventurous. It's sort of like when they have adventure stories, they always start off good and all of these have started off good and they're adventurous.'

Some young readers were aware of the way in which a text is arranged, others may have to be shown.

'It looks like it comes from a story book. Usually in story books, they have the name of the story and the name of the chapter at the top.' (average reader)

Conversation was often mentioned as indicating a story. This third year junior school reader noted:

'It's a story. It's got speech marks because people are talking.'

Conversation has many small clauses; written language often is more abstract. Spoken language does not contain as many content words as does written language. The content words on this page are in fairly frequent use and therefore will not cause great difficulty. When the language becomes more typical of written text, it is noted by one able reader as being unfamiliar and therefore old-fashioned:

'It's about before now – just sounds like it. "A thin high shouldered shadow flickered grotesquely on the wall behind him." You wouldn't use that type of language if it were modern times.'

The close relationship between the language of speech and that used in some children's stories is noted in a response to a page taken from a further story:

'I think it's another story. It says here, "Don't you know...". It's like a dad or mum saying to a child.'

It must be of concern that some less able first-year secondary school readers still did not seem aware of text as a whole. This reader simply notes a single characteristic:

'It seems like a story, the same. Because them speech marks go round.'

An able first-year secondary school reader, however, is very aware of a relationship of register patterning in both reading and writing and, in particular, of greater formality:

'It sounds like a story. Again it's the way it is written. It is written in the third person, I think it's the third person. It starts off as Dad's holiday and it's the sort of thing I write if I am writing a story.'

The danger of simply noting the pattern of a page without really understanding what is being said is suggested in the remarks of a first-year able reader who compares a page from a drama book with a page from a reference book:

'They're both written as plays. They've got the names on the left and they've got the writing on the other side.'

In the fourth year of the secondary school, some less able pupils seemed more aware of the register patterning:

'It reads along as though it's fiction'.

On the other hand, despite all the stories which will have been heard and read by the fourth year of the secondary school, another less able pupil has little awareness of their register patterning:

'It's a story book. It's got pages and numbers'.

Some able readers, however, were aware of integrated language patterning:

'There's constant text and from reading a bit of it, it's written in the way stories are written. For a start, there's conversation.'

'Definitely another story book. I read the first sentence and it is a statement, it's a speech. The way it is written, it's got slang in it. There doesn't seem to be any questions or statements. It's just narrating. There's no diagrams or anything.'

Responses to pages from the expository genre

Books in the *expository* genre are written with the purpose of objective description and explanation as in many history, geography and science text books. When pupils read such books they are reading what Margaret Donaldson (1989) has called, 'the language of systematic thought' (p 24).

Linguists (Halliday, 1985) sometimes refer to 'grammatical metaphor'. Far from being meaningless jargon, this term describes the different way in which formal written language is patterned. This kind of writing is regarded as sophisticated within our culture. Sometimes we condemn it as being meaningless, when we meet it in official documents, for we are aware of writing where the author is distanced from the reader.

An able fourth-year pupil pointed to the remoteness of the language of some text books:

'From reading a bit of it down here, it seems to be written in a friendly manner as well. It seems to be written with a person in mind, sort of to you, whereas some of these other text book ones are sort of written in space.'

Specialists usually distance themselves from the content as they use the language of their subject. As knowledge about subject areas has developed so has the language which expresses those ideas. For instance, there are specific, independent ways of expressing historical and geographical thinking. We do not anticipate that very young readers will grapple with ideas expressed in the form of adult genres but, if children are to proceed to some understanding of the way in which the thinking of subject areas is expressed, then it is important that they are gradually introduced to books which have relevant language patterning.

Eggins et al (1987) have studied history texts. They suggest that historians select, interpret and generalise from facts about the past. Historians often remove people as individuals from their accounts; they create distance between past events and readers by use of formal language. The sequence of time is replaced by frozen time. Formal history texts, which some pupils will be asked to read as they proceed through the secondary school, may well be written in this way.

In the junior school, pupils read simplified history books which may be written as stories. Clearly it is important that pupils recognise the difference between a factual and fictional story. One able third-year junior school reader remarked about two pages from different history books:

'They're both stories that tell you about things but they are in a kind of story sort of way but it's kind of fact. It is written as a story but it tells you things what have happened.'

There is considerable difference between the way in which history and geography books are written. Again Eggins et al note that geographers group and classify where and what places and things are. They analyse and explain how things are caused and how they affect other things. Geographers use technical language as they name and define. Taxonomies are set up to organise the world. These observations are also true of scientific writing which is even more explicit and thus employs precise vocabulary and complexity of grammar. Chapter headings and sub-headings in texts are indicative of the order which geographers and scientists seek to place on the world.

An able fourth-year secondary school pupil noted the different mode of writing on a page from an expository book from the mode of a page from other genres:

'It seems to be a textbook. It's got subject headings, just the things it says are not the sort of thing you'd find in a story book or dictionary.'

This able third-year junior school reader was aware of the implication of different register patterning as she considered a description of hurricanes:

'That's sort of scientific like this one. It's explaining something. The language it uses. You wouldn't in a story, or something like that, say, 'Hurricanes appear over the Caribbean and other parts of the world.'

Sometimes factual books are written in an inappropriate register patterning which is not helpful to the developing reader. An able first-year secondary school reader referred to a page from a book about dinosaurs and expresses relief that the writer had not attempted to write about such a subject in a story genre:

'That's history. It's facts. It's no story line in it. It's realistic rather than silly things like him saying, "Hello" to another dinosaur.'

Rare awareness that language expresses the author's purpose was shown by this average fourth-year secondary school pupil who commented on a page from a book describing computers:

'It's kind of information, yet not. It's more about computers and their word length and it's kind of information but not the information that I would classify with that one (a page from a dictionary). It'll be going into more detail rather than a book telling you a few things, something that was on computers and then it would have different chapters and that would be going into more chapters.'

Pupils' responses to pages from books in the procedural genre

The writer whose purpose is to instruct children in an activity uses a procedural genre as in mathematics books or language activity books. These books are not always as easily understood as we might imagine, for the register patterning of instructions may be complex and, at times, may be that of the expository genre.

The purpose of the writer may not be immediately obvious. For instance, the vocabulary of a work card accompanying a reading scheme indicates, at first glance, that the reader is to think about stories but, in fact, the task for the pupil is to think about writing for different purposes. The card gives written instructions in the form of a list. The reader has to follow these instructions and undertake a writing task in a completely different genre. The format of the page is obviously not that of a narrative but this was not understood by the less able reader who said,

'This is a story sort of one. It's got lots of writing and it says there, "Stories and books".'

Often a science text book is written in the procedural genre. An able first-year secondary school reader notes this:

'They're sort of science experiments; they're actually written in the same way telling you what to do. It's actually explaining what you've got to do and things and telling you what you need and how you've got to do it.'

An average fourth-year secondary school pupil noted the constraints of the patterning of a page from a typing instruction booklet:

'It's giving you information on typewriters but not in great detail. It's sticking to the main points. It's much heavier type and there's two different subjects on about half a side which isn't giving you much room for information.'

Pupils' responses to pages from books in the reference genre

The purpose of the writers of reference books is to provide sequential information about particular subject areas, as in dictionaries or encyclopaedias. There may be overlapping register patterns, as the descriptions of the listed items may be written in an expository genre.

An able first-year secondary school reader noted such a change of patterning in the register of a dictionary:

'That's a dictionary. The words it's talking about are thickly written so it stands out and then it's got sometimes it has a sort of Latin or something and then it explains the word.'

Many books in the reference genre are used by junior school pupils as they undertake projects. Pupils are asked to look up information but they must then be able to cope with the register patterning of the particular item and then, what is even more difficult, translate this into their words! We should never under-estimate the difficulty of the simple command, 'Write it in your own words'!

A dictionary often contains abbreviations which have to be understood and the definitions of the words may be written in a very concise way. Pupils seem to note these linguistic differences with varying degrees of accuracy:

'It's not a story. That looks like dictionary writing, doesn't it down to there.'

We must be sure that readers have clear notions of the field of the text, be it written or graphic. An average first-year secondary school reader described a map of agricultural products as being about history:

'It's maps and that. History is about maps.'

Some fourth-year secondary school less able pupils seemed to have more awareness of writers' purposes. A less able fourth-year pupil described a page from a reference book about fish:

'It's a book about fish. It's not a story book. It's telling you something.'

We cannot be sure that the majority of pupils by the fourth year of the secondary school are as aware of the differences in register pat-terning in a reference book as this pupil:

'A factual book that tells you something in prose. I looked at the first sentence, "This is perhaps the largest barb" but then I knew it wasn't fiction.'

Some implications of these comments

These readers' comments suggest that flexible, competent readers have more developed awareness of the varying register patterning of different genres. Children do not automatically become aware of different register patterns of written language. Some young readers absorb language differences but it would seem that at no stage of schooling can we assume that pupils understand fully the way in which a writer expresses meaning. In fact, we are dealing with matters of linguistic complexity but linguists now have insights into the way language works which are helpful to us.

The notion of genre suggests a basis from which we ourselves may become more aware of register patterning and thus be in a better position to help pupils develop their own awareness. The critics of genre theory insist that such thinking indicates that writing and reading can be taught according to formulae. Such observations misunderstand genre theory. No genre is static, for our culture has evolved and is still evolving ways of expressing meaning through language. Some of these ways or genres are the language of reflection, of imagination; others are ways of thinking; others are the language of power in our society. In fact, genres are language across the curriculum.

The responses of many first-year secondary school readers suggested that they simply categorised different genres as belonging to a particular subject area. Less able fourth-year secondary school pupils continued in the same way but some of the average readers, and most of the able fourth-year readers, described something of the way in which they noted the language was patterned.

As teachers, we should become more aware of how things are written as well as the content of what is written. A particular subject is written about in a certain way. As sophisticated readers, we know this implicitly, but how far can we explain the patterns of writing used by authors?

Only a few able fourth-year secondary school pupils suggested that they had some understanding of the way in which authors' purposes dictate the way in which they pattern language. We have, I believe, a responsibility in the way we help children to think about language and to understand the different ways in which they can use it. We introduce most children to the register patterning of stories effectively. Of course, we must not lose sight of the enormous importance of stories but neither must we neglect the other ways in which writers express meaning. As Margaret Donaldson (1989) explains:

'There is, most fortunately, no incompatibility between developing a love of literature, with all the personal enrichment which that brings, and developing the ways of handling language that favour clear, sustained rational thought. These can – and should – develop side by side, through the school years.' (p 34)

If young readers are to develop flexibility, they must be introduced to the broad canvas of reading different genres. It is equally the responsibility of infant teachers, of junior teachers, and of secondary school subject specialists to have sufficient knowledge of language that will enable them to extend pupils' experience of books in ways which are appropriate to their age and ability.

References

Donaldson, M. (1989) *Sense and sensibility*. University of Reading: Reading and Language Information Center.

Eggins, S., Martin, J. R. and Wignell, P. (1987) *Working papers in linguistics, no 5*, Writing Project Report. Australia; University of Sydney.

Halliday, M. A. K. (1985) *An introduction to functional grammar*. London: Arnold.

Kress, G. (1984) Things children read and things children write. In Unsworth, L., *Reading, writing and spelling*. Proceedings of the 5th Macarthur Reading/Language Symposium, 1984. Sydney: Macarthur Institute of Higher Education.

Martin, J. (1984) *Language, register and genre*: Language Studies Children Writing Reader (ECT 412) Victoria, Australia; Deakin University.

13   Open learning –
an introductory perspective

Bruce A Gillham

Initial thoughts

Whatever I write in this chapter, however interesting, provocative
or occasionally, profound, one thing is certain – I shall still only
be scratching the surface of a fascinating debate.

The trouble is that I cannot begin by defining open learning
without negating the notion that lies at the heart of 'openness'. As
an elusive concept – the subject of debate – it is safe. Wasn't it
G. K. Chesterton who said that he had always suspected men with
open minds because they were only waiting to close them firmly
upon something? It matters little who did say it because it still
encapsulates how I feel about defining open learning. Once defined to our satisfaction – either to a personal or, more dangerous-
ly, an official satisfaction – the concept is closed instead of open.
To find it is to lose it.

Human beings have a pronounced weakness for labels which
amounts to an almost pathological need for certainty. People with
some undefined illness often appear less happy than those con-
firmed in a terrible one! Jerome K Jerome was anxious because,
having scoured the medical dictionary, he had everything *except*
housemaid's knee – why, he pondered, should he be de-
prived of this delicious label? Michael Young's seminal book,
Knowledge and control, explored the way in which knowledge can
be reconstructed and used to fit a vast range of motivations.
Viewed in this light, it is interesting to see how knowledge is
being reconstructed in the field of education and curriculum development. One thing which is currently happening at all levels is
that there is a continuing decline in the level of certainty and
authority with which knowledge is being delivered by teachers.
The whole business of 'making sense' has shifted *from* the bearer

of authoritative messages *to* pupils and students. Learners are increasingly expected to construct *their own* realities from the information and ideas provided. In addition, they are expected to select and incorporate large quantities of information and ideas which they can access from a vast range of possible sources, from their own experience and from the schemas which they have constructed inside their own heads.

Increasingly, we feel that if we *give* our pupils and students the answers we will stop them thinking and stifle their potential for intellectual creativity. Open learning, it seems to me, is part of a broad pedagogical philosophy incorporating notions like uncertainty, flexibility and relativism.

Open learning – a challenge

Open learning then poses a particular challenge to the idea that there is a store of *special* knowledge only available to equally *special* people. Open learning is in diametric opposition to the assumptions implicit in Plato's notion of the *Guardians* – chosen people whose role is to control our destinies.

- *It is a challenge* to an educational system which is run by those who have never 'failed' and in which opportunities and rewards are closed to most.
- *It is a challenge* to the idea of the teacher as the transmitter of authoritative knowledge. It is difficult not to concede that the value of recent *peer teaching* experiments goes far beyond simple knowledge acquisition.
- *It is a challenge* to the subject expert hiding behind an inscrutable expertise and avoiding or undervaluing the role of broader communication in his array of skills.
- *It is a challenge* to the notion that education is about knowledge rather than about learning processes, procedures and skills.
- *It is a challenge* to the system which 'irrelevances' people into under-achievement and denies them satisfaction, fulfillment and self actualisation.
- *It is a challenge* to the *right answer* which bypasses discussion, explanation and alternative views.
- *And, finally, it is a challenge* to an assumption that educators

seem to make at all levels – the assumption that learners arrive naked and naive with little experience and few ideas worthy of exploitation and development during the progress of their learning programmes. Amazingly, this assumption is prevalent in vast numbers of courses clearly designed for individuals with substantial *personal, vocational, professional, industrial,* and *social* experience.

Open learning is then a challenge to a whole series of arrogant, dismissive and parblind perspectives on the educational experiences of individual learners.

So what can be done?

Well, here we are, already some way into a discussion of open learning without a definition and without anything resembling a description of what this elusive pedagogy actually consists of. Perhaps the problem posed by definition can be tackled without too much prescription by trying to clarify the idea through negative statements rather than positive ones. It may be easier to say what open learning *isn't* rather than what it *is*. So we'll concentrate on the characteristics of a learning situation which cause closure. The clear message contained in this sort of exploration is that, if we are going to keep learning *open*, we must side-step all those situational features which tend to close things down.

Avoiding closure

Without trying to rank order the circumstances which close down opportunity or make any claim that this list is exhaustive, we present what follows as a framework for defining the concept of open learning.

Learning is closed by any circumstance which causes the learner to look the other way or fail to notice the opportunity which is being presented.

Learning is closed by underselling what's on offer

This isn't just a question of poor advertising – it is a failure to show and convince the learner of the genuine benefits attached to the course. Why is it worthwhile, how can it be justified and what are the likely pay-offs for the learner? Unless the learner finds convincing answers to such questions, motivation will be reduced. Effective learning is always built on a willingness to be involved.

Learning is closed by the procedures and assumptions of an unsympathetic or unwilling administrative system

All our educational institutions seem to be beset by barriers. In fact, erecting hurdles which defeat all but the best athletes and the most enthusiastic jumpers may often be seen as evidence of *high standards*. The times, dates and organisation of courses – and of schools – seem to run on a very slow and maladaptive clock. Entry criteria frequently exclude many who have the will, energy and need to benefit from what is being offered. The advance of more flexible entry criteria to courses and an increasing recognition of value of non-academic experiences is now, thankfully, beginning to make some headway.

Learning is closed down by high levels of anxiety

Our system revels in stress. Staff development activities in schools, colleges and in higher education frequently seem to generate inadequacy feelings and low morale rather than a genuine improvement in performance. Learners who feel threatened and anxious make little progress following the tunnel vision mapped out for them by their blinkered anxieties.

Learning is closed when the perception of 'work load' proves too much for an individual learner

Our courses often seem to be reliant on enormous slabs of information delivered at an invariable rate to a highly variable clientele. The individual learner, powerless to prevent it, is soon awash with tasks which seem impossible to handle.

Learning is closed by the undisciplined subject expertise of the teacher

There is no doubt that expertise is a gift, an inevitable necessity in any learning situation. But it is often the natural enemy of communication. The subject language of the specialist, and the familiar use of complex ideas, form a barrier of mysteries to the naive learner. Ironically, the expert is often less able to communicate the key ideas of his subject to a naive learner than a more ordinary mortal. The non-expert is more likely to explain carefully as he explores the problems of the subject matter at a level of banality which would be despised by the expert. Expertise undermines the empathetic understanding which any good teacher needs to have with his students.

Learning can be closed down by almost any form of rigidity

Intellectual rigidity, organisational rigidity and an inflexible methodology will all conspire against learners. The preferred patterns and approaches of one learner may be very different from another. One studies best in bed, another sitting at a hard chair in front of a desk. One studies and learns best at night, another is most effective from 9 to 4. One learner thrives in isolated learning situations, another likes working directly with a teacher in a large group. The cards are stacked against any learner who fails to remark and conform to the rigidities around him.

Learning is closed by any unnecessary inconvenience to the learner

It is important to remember that the individuals involved in learning at school, or college, or training in industry, are human beings. If the opportunities offered to them are designed and approached in a way which pays scant attention to their convenience then the learners withdraw, take-up is reduced and the opportunities close down. A perfect example of this is provided by the Open University's core of television-based course time. The unsocial hours of screening has for many years taxed the willpower of even the most avid students. The low level of priority given to these elements of the course by students has drastically reduced the contribution which they are able to make. The advent of the video recorder has certainly eased the situation but it has not solved the problem. But think positively about what would happen if, when the student reached the correct point in a course booklet, he came across a red button conveniently placed in the margin bearing the caption – *Press this button when you wish to view the programme for this part of the Unit, the pictures will then appear within the small box just below this button.* The answer is that, like Alice when faced with the label *Eat me!*, the temptation to press the button would be irresistible.

Learning is closed by the facts of history

We educate children and young people in schools and colleges, in classrooms and lecture rooms. We operate with a range of facilities which represent a past view of the conditions under which learning *should* take place. We know that for every individual the design of the environment is a crucial part of learning success. For many learners opportunities are closed because the circumstances surrounding them do not help them to achieve success. If learners had the power to construct *their own* learning environment, the situation would be radically different.

Learning is closed by a whole range of apparently self evident, unchallengeable facts and realities

For example, it is highly questionable whether the conventional *class group* structure is the optimum arrangement for learning. The standard class size, the conventional arrangement of the working day, and all that sitting behind desks or in serried ranks in lecture theatres which we impose on learners, are all likely to defeat rather than encourage learning.

Learning is closed by the relationships existing between the partners in learning

The use of the word *partners* may be a misnomer here because the authoritative relationship between the teacher and the learner is still the dominant model. However, there is now a progressive movement to turn the teacher at all levels into a facilitator who manages and resources learning and provides knowledge, wisdom, discussion and friendship during the learning process.

Learning is closed by learner passivity

The passive learner is typified by the text book reader. The vast majority of text books still make no physical or practical demands of their readers. There are no challenges, no problems, no experiments, no action. The text book is a monologue – and many lectures and lessons are too! For the student, passivity leads either to exhaustion and sleep or, alternatively, it generates a curriculum which goes on under the desk.

Learning is closed by a lack of empathy with the learner

Learning is also closed down by a whole range of feelings, activities and technical procedures involved in the learning process. For example, it can be closed down by *an inadequate level of feedback about performance*, by *the style of assessment* used in the educational process, by a *lack of humour and an inadequate recognition of the humanity of the learner* and by the *subject territoriality of many people in our profession*.

The last point perhaps requires some further explanation. Human beings seem to have a weakness for knowledge delivered in conventional bundles and within conventional frameworks. This has caused a failure in learning because the real world is not so conveniently parcelled out. As a result, the learner is not helped to make many of the natural connections *between* the various knowledge bundles or *subjects*. Areas of enquiry which *cross* conventional boundaries have been singularly slow to develop. Thus, *language across the curriculum, multicultural studies*, and *health education* have all experienced problems of credibility. And anyone trying to develop a *humanities curriculum* in an holistic way will have stumbled into the entrenchments dug by all the specialist *subject area interests* resisting what they see as a hostile invasion.

Towards a definition?

So where does this rather negative discussion get us? The answer is that it allows us a glimpse of what is meant by the term *open learning* and to hazard at least a tentative definition.

Our first attempt at definition is to say that:

'an *open learning* approach is any approach to learning which is systematically designed to avoid closure and seeks to open up educational accessibility.'

More descriptively, we might say that:

'an *open learning* system is one which puts the individual learner at the centre of things. It is sensitive to the learner's motivations, anxieties, convenience, preferred study mode and language capacity. It is flexible, in terms of organisation, workload, work pacing and timing. The learning materials which accompany an open learning system are precisely targeted at particular learners, are learner active, personal, friendly, and conversational in style. In addition, the open learning system is one which tries to create learning materials which circumvent the communication trap posed by subject expertise and takes steps to tackle the unhelpful legacy of buildings, structures, procedures and assumptions passed on by tradition.'

And in conclusion

In conclusion, it is obvious that open learning is not new *and* that it will never be totally achievable. It is an ideal notion towards which we are trying to make progress. We need to achieve a more universal provision of educational opportunity. We want to be able to deliver education – and training – *whenever* and *wherever* it is needed, and *in a way* which recognises the true nature of the context.

Open learning is associated with several important principles:

1 *the individual's right to education* – the contention being that education is about 'needs' and 'access' rather than about 'selection' and 'comparison';
2 *the dignity of the individual* – involving a move towards a less authoritarian teaching style and a greater empathy with the learner;
3 *the central importance of education in social development* – including the ability of the system to respond to all sorts of commercial, social, intellectual and environmental changes;
4 *the belief that education is about processes, models and ways of doing things* – the tyranny of the fact laden curriculum is not behind us, of course, but many of the movements we see around us in the system, GCSE, TVEI, education for capability, and so on, all give us grounds for optimism.

Openness is harder to achieve than we once thought. Our system still finds it easier to close doors or police them in an intimidating way than to put out the 'welcome mat'.

14 Open learning and basic skills provision for adults

Gill Dempsey

In this chapter my aims are:

1 To look at the national context for the development of open learning within basic skills provision for adults, and to discuss:
   (i)   the current level and nature of provision in literacy and basic skills;
   (ii) recent initiatives in open learning and basic skills;
   (iii) basic skills and computer-based learning;
   (iv) links with employers – national initiatives;
   (v) student accreditation.
2 To focus on the experience of one of the newly-established centres, looking particularly at:
   (i)   the setting-up phase;
   (ii) organising learning and the role of the tutor;
   (iii) use of new technology

The national context

(i) Level and nature of provision in literacy and basic skills

The past two decades have seen a remarkable growth in the provision of learning opportunities for adults seeking literacy/basic skills support. Many will associate the start of any significant provision with the 'On the Move' BBC series of 1975, and this was indeed the beginning of the widespread national development of provision for adults, which had previously existed only in very isolated pockets.

In 1973 it was estimated that only 5000 adults were receiving help with reading and writing in the whole of England and Wales. Although a steadily increasing number of students were seeking help through 1974, only about 17,000 were receiving tuition at the beginning of 1975. Just one year later in February 1976, 53,000 adult students were being taught and, by 1978, some 125,000 students had been helped to improve their reading and writing. By 1985 well over 300,000 students had received tuition.

There are over 100,000 adults receiving literacy/basic skills tuition in 1990, and provision is made by every LEA in England and Wales. Volunteers continue to be an important characteristic of provision, though the predominant model is the 'two hour group', probably co-ordinated by a paid tutor.

(ii)   Recent initiatives in open learning and basic skills

1988 saw the beginning of significant developments in the provision of flexible learning opportunities for adults seeking literacy and basic skills support. This began with the Inner City projects, a joint ALBSU/DES/Welsh Office initiative to establish a network of inner city centres throughout England and Wales. The first of these centres were open by March 1988, and there are likely to be a total of eleven finally in operation. These include centres in Leeds, Birmingham, Bristol and Tower Hamlets, and the locations for the centres include community buildings and 'street front' sites such as shops and a former bank. After the start of this initiative, an Education Support Grant of three million pounds was announced to establish further open learning centres to a similar brief, and 57 of these centres have now been approved to get under way from April 1989, with a further three projects to be based in Wales. Thus, by the beginning of the 1990s there will be a network of such centres in England and Wales, and it is envisaged that they will make a significant impact on both the way in which literacy/basic skills is delivered and the scale of learning opportunities on offer. (When it is considered that the expenditure on literacy/basic skills in 1986–7 was estimated at fifteen to eighteen million pounds, clearly the open learning initiatives represent a significant increase in the resourcing of literacy/basic skills, and it is hoped that this will be reflected in a 'quantum leap' in the number of students in provision.) The shared characteristics of both the inner city centres and the ESG funded centres include:

- the provision of a range of learning opportunities (eg drop-in, learning by appointment, workshop-based provision, short courses);

● the integration of new technology into learning programmes;
● collaboration with local employers to design provision that reflects their needs.

It is hoped that what will emerge from the open learning centres will be principles of good practice when providing literacy/basic skills on a flexible basis, addressing such issues as:

● how to assess and evaluate progress when there are flexible patterns of attendance;
● how to plan integrated learning programmes that use a 'repertoire' of learning tools;
● how to support students with basic learning needs.

(iii) Basic skills and computer-based learning

The Adult Literacy and Basic Skills Unit (ALBSU) has funded development work to foster the use of computers in basic skills, both through projects which have designed specific pieces of software and through supporting staff and curriculum development that encourages the integration of the computer into the curriculum, for example through the use of the wordprocessor and database. This latter work, particularly, has proved an important backdrop to the use of computers in the open learning centres.

(iv) Links with employers

It is likely that, with the fall in unemployment and population decline, literacy/basic skills in the workplace could see considerable expansion in the 1990s because of the need to update and retrain the existing workforce.

The current major national initiative in this area is the Workbase National Project. This project is implementing the strategies developed by work within the London Division of the National Union of Public Employees. The national project is now working with a number of employers throughout the UK. It aims to implement the strategies first developed by the London based project on a national basis by setting up basic education courses on a paid release basis, assessing the literacy/basic skills needs of an organisation through survey work, and encouraging a co-operative strategy between employers, unions and educationalists to promote literacy/basic skills.

Workbase has provided important 'models' for work with employers, for translation into an open learning context, and, though at an early stage, links between open learning centres and employers are developing.

(v)   Student accreditation

It is hoped that the open learning centres will prove the focus of support for adults wishing to participate in the Basic Skills Accreditation Initiative, which got under way in 1989.

The Basic Skills Accreditation Initiative is a collaborative venture jointly sponsored by the Department of Education and Science, the Department of Employment and the BBC. It brings together the Training Agency, the Adult Literacy and Basic Skills Unit and the BBC. It aims to recruit and offer new learning opportunities to a wide range of adults with literacy and numeracy needs. The focus for the initiative is the development of new certificates in communication skills and numeracy. Between Autumn 1989 and Spring 1990 the BBC broadcast a number of radio and television programmes on literacy and basic skills.

The certificates are being developed at four levels and it is intended that they should be related to the framework being developed by the National Council for Vocational Qualifications and reflect an individual's competence in context. The first two series of television programmes will deal with communication skills and will reflect the first two levels of the communication skills certificate. Level 1 can be described as encompassing communication skills (reading, writing, talking and listening) which meet basic and familiar demands of life and work. Level 2 reflects competence at craft and junior levels of employment and in meeting demands of life and work in familiar and unfamiliar situations.

A second stage of programmes from October 1990 will concentrate on numeracy and a numeracy certificate, as well as the higher levels of the communication skills certificate, will be developed to coincide with these broadcasts. Radio broadcasts will supplement the television programmes.

The experience of one centre – Burton Road Open Learning Centre, Leeds LEA

The Open Learning Centre in Leeds is the longest established of the ten inner city pilot centres. It opened in October 1988.

The centre is based on the ground floor of a free standing building formerly part of a school, now divided into continuing education and training, in an area south of the city centre. Burton Road is in the middle of a residential inner city area, with mixed high rise and terraced housing stock. There is a high proportion of residents from ethnic minority communities.

Though some other educational/training provision is in the building, the centre is fairly self contained, being close to the main entrance and having its own office and teaching/learning area. Also housed on the group floor are the creche and the canteen, both fairly well used by students.

Setting up

The project workers were faced with the challenge of equipping the centre with appropriate technology and paper based resources and making decisions about the arrangements and storage of materials to encourage maximum accessibility and enable students to move from one learning resource to another. Within four weeks the centre was equipped with a range of hardware including BBC and Amstrad computers and video, a large bank of worksheet materials stored in open shelving and grouped into areas of study such as punctuation, report writing etc. The rationale behind categorisation of resources is under constant review by centre staff.

Leeds has an excellent track record in resourcing basic skills and supporting innovatory work, and there is a considerable pool of practitioner expertise within the authority that the centre has been able to draw on. The service provided by the centre has been enhanced by the additional staff resources put into the centre by the authority.

With a mode of learning that aims to offer as much flexibility as possible to the student, it is important that tutors share a common philosophy and approach, and a priority has been given to encouraging all staff to contribute to the centre's working philosophy.

The section below summarises the approach of the centre to:

- the role of tutor;
- modes of delivery;
- student progress;
- use of new technology.

(ii)　*The role of tutor in open learning centres*

Responsibility for learning is shared between student/tutor/ volunteer tutor. There is no room for the traditional active teacher/ passive student role in an open learning situation.

The role of tutor is to: –

- negotiate;
- diagnose problems;
- find starting points;
- direct/promote self access;
- encourage self assessment/independence;
- facilitate learning;
- give information (within brief);
- pass on to appropriate agency if necessary;
- maintain 'control' in a positive way.

Tutors are expected to teach a wide range of subject areas and levels within one session (which is very demanding). They need to be much more open in the way they work. Tutors also have to liaise with other tutors very closely; communication between staff is very important. As a result, there is more emphasis on team teaching which acknowledges and respects the expertise of other tutors and the strengths and weaknesses of tutors with different groups.

As tutors are much more dependent on resources and accessing those resources quickly, they need to identify gaps in resources and ways of filling them. Tutors are also more involved with administration; record keeping has a new level of importance.

Modes of delivery are as follows:

- 1:1 tuition, individually negotiated;
- group tuition for new technology/creative writing/ESOL on a regular basis;

- group tuition on a floating basis, as need arises, on a variety of topics, exam related plus as a result of perceived needs;
- group tuition for groups with specially defined needs, eg, ET trainees in new technology;
- distance learning – 'home study'.

(iii) *Use of new technology*

Why use new technology in adult basic education? Computer-assisted learning/word processing is used:

- to aid language development;
- to build word attack skills;
- to aid proof reading and transcription skills;
- to teach particular skills, eg, punctuation/spelling;
- to reinforce teaching by other more traditional methods;
- to provide satisfaction in a final product;
- to aid computer literacy;
- to provide an adult medium for learning in an area without previous experiences of failure.

The technology housed by the centre is under constant heavy use. Many students seek a basic grasp of word processing techniques, either as precursor to vocational training or as an extension to developing their literacy skills. Some students use individual pieces of software to practise specific literacy/numeracy skills.

The centre is also currently using a computer based system for recording and monitoring student attendance, which involves students 'signing in' using a bar code system.

The Leeds centre has consistently had a role to play in delivering basic skills to trainees on the government funded employment training programme. The negotiation of specific short course provision for local employers is beginning with a basic keyboard course for employees at a local engineering firm.

In conclusion, I maintain that, although the development of initiatives in open learning and basic skills are currently at an early stage, the indications are that this form of provision could produce a significant increase in the number of adults receiving basic skills tuition, as well as extending the basic skills curriculum.

15   Open learning and teacher education

John E Merritt

The need for a more open approach to learning in teacher education has become increasingly apparent in recent years. The Open
University has for some time been meeting part of this need. In
addition, many of the INSET courses provided by other institutions are now much more open than they were. The need for an
even greater degree of openness, however, is reflected in the
widespread support that is being given to school based approaches
to teacher education.

There are, of course, any number of ways in which we might
make education more, or less, 'open' – and different reasons for
doing so. This chapter looks at some of these different aspects of
openness and considers why they are particularly important in
teacher education. In each case, it goes on to look at some of the
possible practical implications.

The chapter also describes an approach which is designed to
make open education for teachers both professionally attractive
and more widely accepted. It provides a system of modular credits
for teachers pursuing their own professional development activities
in their own way in their own schools. The first of these modules
focuses on English and the Whole School Curriculum. This particular module is described in the final section of this paper.

Aspects of open learning and the needs of teachers

One very convenient way of looking at openness is to ask the
investigative questions: Who? What? When? Where? How? – and,
in each case, Why?

Who: who is allowed in?

Access to education is often restricted to people who have appropriate entry qualifications. In open learning, however, it is assumed that a general feeling of *need*, appropriate previous *experience* and a sufficient amount of *enthusiasm* will usually compensate for lack of formal qualifications. Certainly, this is the assumption made by the Open University – and its many thousands of successful graduates bear testimony to the soundness of that assumption.

In the case of teachers, the *need* has been created by the Education Reform Act: teachers now need open access to all kinds of opportunities of professional development. Teachers are certainly not lacking in professional *experience* and if they are not currently *enthusiastic* then that is simply a challenge to INSET providers to make their courses more attractive – and relevant – so that teachers really want to take them.

In the Cumbria project, *Classroom Practice and the National Curriculum*, there is open access for any group of teachers who wish to work together on their own school-based in-service activities. It is open only to groups of teachers, rather than individual teachers, because it is based, essentially, on a whole school approach to development.

What: what must they cover?

The longer the course the more likely it is that some people will find themselves doing work they do not actually need: the priorities of the student are not necessarily the same as those of the course designer. For open learning, courses need to be broken down into smaller chunks, or modules, so that students are able to choose those parts that are most important from their own point of view.

We must bear in mind, however, that all courses, long or short, are put together so that they can provide for a gradual development of closely related skills and/or concepts. In modular courses it may be necessary to allow for some way of helping people to do this for themselves.

Teachers, particularly those in primary schools, have to cover a wide spectrum of knowledge and skills. Whatever they do study has to be in line with the priorities of the school as well as their own personal/professional priorities. There must therefore be considerable flexibility and openness in any kind of in-service provision.

Over and above this, teachers have to organise what they learn in order to provide a curriculum that is 'balanced and broadly based':

(2)   The curriculum for a maintained school satisfies the requirements of this section if it is a balanced and broadly based curriculum which –

(a)   promotes the spiritual, moral, cultural, mental and physical development of pupils at the school and of society; and

(b)   prepares such pupils for the opportunities, responsibilities and experiences of adult life.

Education Reform Act 1988, Chapter 40. Part 1, Schools, Chapter 1.

This curriculum must also make sense to the particular children they happen to teach. It would be unsatisfactory, therefore, simply to provide isolated modules. There must clearly be some very direct help for teachers as they constantly strive to impose some kind of overall pattern on their own learning.

In the Cumbria project, *Classroom Practice and the National Curriculum*, the modular course structure has been designed to provide an enabling framework for school-based initiatives over a period of six terms. These in-service activities can be pursued not only by teachers with different interests but also by teachers with different responsibilities.

The project offers a series of modules at Certificate Level. These will count as Level One in a Diploma course that is currently being validated. A series of matching modules are to be provided at Level Two. These are for groups of teachers who wish to continue with the same kinds of in-service activities at a more advanced level in order to gain the Diploma. Eventually, it is hoped to provide an M.Ed course so that groups of teachers can work together at different levels on common problems.

If teachers are already providing a curriculum that is 'balanced and broadly based', it could be argued that there is no need for any further help in developing an overall framework. Presumably, they already have one. Their activities in each module introduce no serious discontinuities because they are simply a further evaluation and development of the school's own current policy and practice. Any new ideas that are brought in are simply a means of throwing further light on ideas that are perfectly coherent already.

This, however, would be a slightly optimistic scenario. Help is therefore provided for teachers to relate what they do for the National Curriculum to the demands of the Whole School Curriculum as set out in the Education Reform Act. Some indication of the kind of help that is offered is provided in Table A. There are three options from which to choose. These, together with the general course structure, are illustrated in Table B. The main thrusts of the respective options are as follows:

(i)   Classroom practice and the National Curriculum

In this option teachers can concentrate on any area of curriculum they choose. In Module 1, special attention is given to English in cross-curricular activities both at Level 1 and at Level 2. In Module 3, extra attention is given to Maths and Science.

(ii)   School-based INSET and the National Curriculum

This option is for teacher coordinators whose task is to foster professional development by enabling colleagues to develop their professional skills to meet the demands of the National Curriculum within the general context provided by the Education Reform Act.

(iii)   School and community and the National Curriculum

This option is aimed at schools in which there is an emphasis on relating to parents and to others in the community within the context of the National Curriculum and the Education Reform Act in general.

There are three main considerations in this third module:

- the need to take full advantage of a valuable additional resource;
- the need to help children to relate their curriculum to the realities of everyday life in their own communities;
- the need to provide opportunities for parents in the community to develop a much better understanding of the work that really goes on in schools so that, as well informed parents and citizens, they can make a much more substantial contribution to progress in education.

Table A *Perspectives on the whole school curriculum*

The following list provides one way of checking the range of topics or activities you may wish to include in your Whole School Curriculum. Start with any of the following headings then explore the possibilities for cross-curricular enrichment by checking each of the other headings in the table.

Self-reliance (= What do I really need/want – and what can I do about it?)	**Active Citizenship** (= What sort of world do I really need/want – and what can I do about it?)
Health and personal fitness	*Ecology and environmental quality*
Physical health	Natural ecology
Mental health	Man-made environment
Hazards	Hazards
Sex	Leisure pressures
Culture and self-awareness	*Culture and community awareness*
Art; dance; drama; music	Galleries; theatres; pageants
English; modern languages	Schools; colleges; universities
History; geography; social sciences	Clubs; learned societies
Maths; science; technology	Libraries; museums; exhibitions
Pastimes; games; hobbies	Clubs; associations
PE; outdoor pursuits	Leisure centres; stadia; open spaces
RE; humanism	Places of worship/communion

Economics and personal resources
Supplies and facilities
Technology (including design)
Cash and services

Networks and personal relationships
Home and family
School and community
Clubs
People in need
Other people

Information and personal intelligence
Investigation
Evaluation
Application
Communication

Social context and personal development
Personal history and context
Personal achievements
Personal potential
Religious beliefs and personal values
Personal priorities

Economics and industrial enterprise
Raw materials and infrastructure
Industry and commerce
Finance and public services

Networks and social relationships
Community groups and voluntary services
Statutory bodies and political groups
Trades/professions
Firms and consumers
Other communities

Information and public intelligence
Investigative groups/agencies
Interest groups
Information sources/services
Information technology

Political context and community development
My society's history and context – records
My society's current achievements – data
My society's potential – guesstimates
Religious systems & social values – freedom of expression
Social priorities – representation

Table B

Curriculum option	Teacher coordinator option	School and community option

Level 1

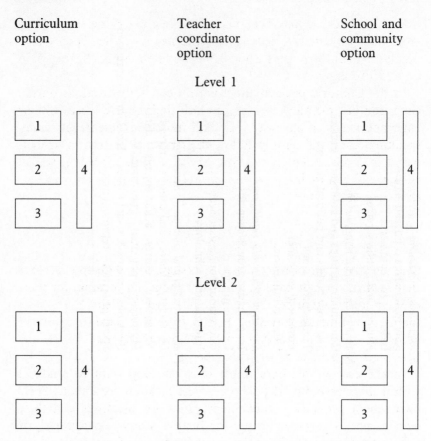

Level 2

On all three grounds, the answer to the 'Who' question at the beginning of this paper must eventually include not just teachers but parents, and others in the community, for education is not truly open until they too are working partners in the educational process. Credits are provided for completing a module. Any teacher who successfully completes four modules at Level One is awarded a Certificate, and satisfactory completion of four further modules at Level Two leads to the award of a Diploma in Advanced Studies in Education. At each level, three of the modules can be completed in successive terms. The fourth module is a dissertation.

When: when can they do it?

Course time-tables may bear very little relation to personal time-tables and priorities. For teachers, the needs of the school come first and their own professional development must be fitted in around this.

In the Cumbria project, there are no course restrictions on the allocation of time and teachers can link their course work to their emerging needs in any way they find most convenient. Generally speaking, they will simply follow their normal pattern of school-based in-service meetings during 'directed time'. Their practical work is done in their own classroom, or in the school, on whatever area they have chosen to develop.

Where: where can they do it?

One big advantage of the Open University and the Open College is that students do not have to go to any particular location for most of their study activities. Obviously, this saves students from wasting a lot of time on travelling to and from the place of study. In addition, however, a classroom or lecture room may not be the best place to pursue a particular study.

In the case of teachers, most of what they want to study is within the classroom, the school or the local environment. Their own school provides a convenient venue for meetings and their own home a convenient place for further study – particularly if this further study can be made easier by means of materials which are carefully designed for learning at a distance. In the Cumbria project, some distance learning booklets are provided for sharing within the school whilst others are designed for private study.

How: how can they do it?

The structured lecture format is of limited value – although it has its uses. Most tutors these days lecture as little as possible and try to help their students to discover their own most effective approaches to learning. This, in itself, is a move away from tutor-dominated learning.

For teachers this kind of openness is, or should be, part of their

Figure 15.1 *Weeky routine*

Step 1:   Deciding what to cover

• review possibilities
• decide priorities

Step 2:   Planning the week's work

• review resources and context
• decide strategies

Step 3:   Classroom application

• put plans into action
• observe

Step 4:   Looking back and moving on

• reflect and record
• share with colleagues

own everyday practice with their own pupils. In the Cumbria project, teachers are invited to draw on their own teaching experience when they look at their own learning strategies. They are encouraged to work together in identifying their individual and collective in-service needs, to design their own ways of working, to manage their own learning and to evaluate the learning process as well as the product. This is part of their weekly routine throughout the course (Fig 15.1).

A Course Booklet sets out the pattern of activities for the whole term. Each week, teachers are invited to evaluate their work from the point of view of the particular cross-curricular perspective provided in the Course Booklet for the particular module. The teachers themselves then decide what aspects of their work they want to develop. The course content is thus left entirely open and teachers can spend as much or as little time as they need on any particular topic or area.

They begin by drawing on their own collective experience and expertise. The school's own teacher coordinator then arranges for professional sharing with colleagues in other schools where necessary. The coordinators in different schools also work together to organise a support network of teachers with more specialised interests and/or expertise. They can then 'top up' by calling on outside expertise on a consultancy basis where necessary.

There is also an IT-INSET element (Ashton et al, 1983; Marsh, C. J., 1985). Where this can be arranged, a tutor and a group of students from the College work in the school for one day a week for one term as members of the classroom team. Both tutor and students help the teachers to develop their work in any way that seems most appropriate to all concerned – taking groups of children, undertaking preparatory work of various kinds, helping with evaluation and making themselves generally useful.

English and the Whole School Curriculum

Throughout all the documents on English and the National Curriculum there are constant references to 'purpose', 'audience' and 'context'. There are also frequent references to the importance of English in personal and social education and an emphasis on the teaching of English in cross-curricular activities. This gives powerful support to those teachers who prefer to see English developing as an organic part of other activities.

The first module in the Cumbria project is concerned with English and the Whole School Curriculum. In this module, the course work supports a wholistic approach to the teachers' own learning. It invites teachers to evaluate their classroom practices using 'purpose', 'context' and 'audience' as fundamental categories in the first instance. Only then are they invited to look more closely at any technical elements – in so far as they are immediately relevant.

These valuation and development activities are carried out under four broad headings:

1 Personal purposes and self-reliance

The emphasis here is on enabling children to define their own purposes and priorities and to become more self-reliant in managing their own learning. Teachers are therefore asked to evaluate the opportunity they provide for children to engage in each of the following activities:

Goal setting

(= What exactly do I need to find out [or do] – and why is this important?)

Planning

(= What will I need to get, or use – and how?)

Implementing

(= How am I doing – and how can I do it better?)

Developing

(= Is that what I wanted – and what could I do better next time?)

2 Common purposes and co-operation

In this activity, teachers are invited to adopt a similar approach to that described above. In this case, however, they are invited to look at the opportunities they provide for children to take account of other people's needs and purposes, other people's preferred plans, other people's preferred ways of working and other people's reflections on what they have done. Here, the teacher is looking at the opportunities they provide for co-operative learning of various kinds.

Although children are commonly arranged in groups in the classroom, they usually spend a good deal of their time working on their own. In this activity, teachers are provided with a framework within which group processes may be seen to operate. This is intended to encourage teachers to develop their own ways of stimulating a richer variety of language activities, with sensitivity to audience as the important factor.

3 Context and audience, roles and responsibilities

In the previous two stages, teachers have been looking at basic principles. At this stage they are required to look at the operation of these principles within a greater variety of situations. They are asked to look at the different kinds of audience that their children are able to address and to seek to widen the range wherever possible. This would include, for example, the practice of older children writing for younger children, children co-operating with parents (eg, in the production of story tapes for other children), and various kinds of contacts with other people in the community.

4 Cross-curricular planning

Now, teachers are asked to review their curriculum priorities and to think about the extent to which they are satisfying that most fundamental requirement of the Education Reform Act – the need for a curriculum that is 'balanced and broadly based'. This is not, however, approached simply by looking at the list of subjects in the National Curriculum and that miscellaneous collection of cross-curricular themes which are scattered throughout the current literature. Instead, teachers are asked to consider the extent to which they are actually enabling children to cope with the realities of the everyday world. Table A (pp 138–9) provided an indication of how teachers might approach this particular aspect.

The language children need will obviously be determined by the range of issues they cover in the curriculum. The purpose of this activity, therefore, is to encourage teachers to think about their own priorities with regard to the curriculum, but to define these in relation to the real priorities of everyday life rather than the academic abstractions and ad-hoc formulations of so much writing on curriculum policy and practice.

Concluding comment

In the final analysis, perhaps, what we really mean by openness is our recognition that the student is more important than any particular collection of courses or organisation of course content. Our task is to help students, in this case, teachers, to become more adept at defining their own learning needs and priorities, to organise their own learning, to manage their own learning – and to be scrupulous in reflecting on what they have learnt. Naturally, this is what we are primarily concerned with in the classroom. In adopting this general perspective, teachers can then gradually focus down on those particular aspects of English that are clearly of greatest relevance in whatever ensues.

All of this is merely an extension of what we normally do in our own everyday lives – and an extension of the behaviour that led to our own development of competence in language development from an early age! When we view English teaching as the teaching of a variety of skills, we look at language development through the wrong end of the telescope.

Of course, none of this is new. We are simply saying that we need to teach children (and teachers) – not subjects.

References

Ashton, P. M. E., Henderson, E. S., Merritt, J. E. & Mortimer, D. J. (1983) *Teacher education in the classroom: initial and inservice*. London: Croom Helm.
Marsh, C. J. (1985) *A study of initial training – inservice education and training for teachers (IT-INSET) in the United Kingdom*: Report of the Association of Commonwealth Universities Senior Travelling Fellowship. Murdoch, Western Australia: Murdoch University.

16   GCSE media studies – the way forward?

David Davies

The purpose of this paper is threefold: first, to review the progress made to date in the study of the media in schools; second, to examine some of the key concepts of GCSE media studies as it is taught at present and third, to discuss some possible strategies for the survival of media studies or media education within the context of the National Curriculum. The question mark at the end of the title of my talk is deliberate, partly because I am suggesting only possible strategies for the future of media studies and partly because I sense that many teachers and educationalists in the media field do now feel that a question mark hangs over the future of the subject. I trust that it is only a question mark and not the sword of Damocles.

The background

First, to review the progress of media studies to date. It has been a considerable success story, without a doubt. Len Masterman, Lecturer in Education at Nottingham University, convenor of the first two GCSE media studies conferences in 1988 and 1989 and a considerable influence on the development of the subject, gives a useful summary of the history of attitudes to the media in educational circles in his book *Teaching the Media* (Comedia, 1985). He demonstrates that the attitude has shifted from outright Leavisite opposition to the supposed downgrading of standards involved in any consideration of the media or popular culture in general (via enthusiasm for certain styles of film-making, as seen in the introduction of subjects such as 'film studies' to the curriculum) to the present situation of an almost complete acceptance of the validity of media studies as an established area of the curriculum.

Early critics of the media such as F. R. Leavis and Denys

Thompson in their influential work *Culture and Environment* felt that literature could be used as a kind of bulwark to defend students against the inevitably corrupting influence of the mass media:

'Many teachers of English who have become interested in the possibilities of training taste and sensibility must have been troubled by accompanying doubts. What effect can such training have against the multitudinous counterinfluences – films, newspapers, advertising – indeed the whole world outside the classroom? Yet the very conditions that make literary education look so desperate are those which make it more important than ever before; for in a world of this kind – and a world that changes so rapidly – it is on literary tradition that the office of maintaining continuity must rest.'

The view of media as an influence on pupils' lives which had to be countered remained a significant attitude amongst many teachers, certainly until the 1960s.

When attitudes began to change, they did so only in relation to *parts* of the media. Many teachers of English in schools became interested in the possibilities of film as a medium and courses in film studies or, later, television studies, began to appear. Len Masterman wrote a book called *Teaching Television* for teachers who were adopting this kind of single-medium approach; it is an approach which he, in common with most other media teachers, now repudiates as too limited in scope, particularly at a time when a single organisation such as Rupert Murdoch's News International company extends its tentacles into many different branches of the media.

There were other problems with the single-medium approach as practised in some schools in the 1960s and 1970s. The courses were seldom given the recognition implied by 'O' level status and as a consequence were seen in some schools, rightly or wrongly, as a 'soft option' subject for the less academically-gifted, leading to mode 3 CSE qualifications. I have heard one media studies teacher referring without bitterness to a general dismissal of his subject by the majority of teachers in his school as being 'only for the noddies'.

The fact that the subject was often taught by only one subject specialist in schools also led to difficulties. The enthusiasm of the teacher concerned was sometimes offset by the fact that he or she was hidebound in approach by a background in one particular area, whether it be English, technology, history etc. There was the problem of what media teachers have christened the 'technicist' approach – the tendency to concentrate on the technology involved at the expense of theory. There was also the problem of the enthusiast for one medium who found difficulties in converting what had been a 'hobby'-like enthusiasm into a genuine educational approach.

Finally, the crucial area of 'values' has been a perennial problem for media studies teachers. The legacy of Leavisite beliefs in a tradition of shared values led to an over-emphasis in the 1960s and, to a lesser extent, in the 1970s on an accepted canon, particularly in the traditionally elitist area of film studies. Films by foreign directors were acceptable, but a Western film, for example, even if directed by John Huston, was suspect almost by reason of its popularity. Len Masterman has described the way in which Roland Barthes' book *Mythologies* was a liberating influence for media teachers in the 1970s in the way in which it elevated even the most mundane item such as a plate of steak and chips into a social symbol or sign. To take a comparable example from television, games shows need not now be considered as of negligible significance; they could be seen as essential signifiers of the values of the media and the way people perceived them.

For all these reasons and others, including the expansion and development of media education in higher education which was creating a generation of young 'media literate' teachers, the concept of a unified subject called 'media studies' began to appear on school timetables. The simultaneous advent of the new GCSE examination with syllabuses for media studies meant that the subject could now be taught across the ability range, bringing it out of its ghetto and helping to realise its full potential for the first time.

The present situation

Moving on to my second theme of the present state of GCSE media studies and its 'key concepts', four of the five examining groups in England and Wales currently offer syllabuses in the subject. There is no space here to describe the features of all four syllabuses, but I will attempt to describe the common concepts which are present in them.

The first point is that the syllabuses are conceptual in approach rather than content-led, and as such are very much in line with the general principles of the GCSE examination. Each of the four syllabuses gives different names to these so-called 'key concepts' (this is unfortunate – it would be a valuable task at some stage to devise a common approach to terminology among the syllabuses, but I am certainly not offering to do so!). The following five concepts are, however, basic to all four syllabuses and form the intellectual framework for the subject: media language, media audiences, genre, institutions and representation, and I would like to take a brief look at each of these concepts in turn.

Media language

The concept of media language posits that the media has a language which can be learned in the same way that a written language is learned. You can therefore become media-literate if you understand the media's 'forms and conventions', just as you become literate in a written language.

For this reason media language is usually taught at the beginning of a media studies course in order to familiarise pupils with the forms and conventions of the media. It usually involves pupils in the acquisition of a new vocabulary of terms. To take a straightforward example, pupils will learn to differentiate between the terms *denotation* and *connotation* when considering a photograph. The *denotation* of the photograph will give pupils the straightforward information of what is in the photograph. The *connotation* of the photograph will give pupils an understanding of the associations connected with the symbols in the photograph, the 'positioning' of the people or objects in the frame, whether the image has been 'cropped' (ie selectively cut to give a partial view only of what was originally taken). At a time when advertisers are concentrating as never before on perfecting a visual approach in order to get their message across and when the government is making a determined effort at news management, the need for a basic media literacy among pupils has never been greater.

Media audiences

Once pupils have acquired some understanding of the terms employed by both media professionals and media educators, they are freer and more competent to look at other areas of the media. The concept of media audiences is obviously important to any student of the mass media since by its definition it is attempting to appeal to a large audience and the ways in which it attempts to do this are obviously of legitimate interest to the student.

Examples of the kinds of questions which media studies students are encouraged to ask about the concept of audience are: Who are the audience? How are products designed to appeal to audiences? What sort of people watch what kinds of programmes? They would be encouraged to undertake surveys among their classmates, family and strangers to determine which programmes are watched, which magazines etc are read. They would also be encouraged to ask themselves a question which is fundamental to media studies theory: Who sets the agenda? In other words, who decides what the audience wants, into which categories they should be divided – questions of gender and race are raised here – who *makes* the audience for the mass media?

Genre

Consideration of the concept of audience leads naturally into the related question of genre. The concept of Media Genre can be considered separately for each of the media that are being studied. In television, for example, soap operas, games shows etc can be studied (this can lead to the accusation from parents that it is no part of education to watch *Eastenders* in the classroom); in films, westerns, science fiction etc can be examined and in pop music the various divisions such as heavy metal, reggae, hip-hop and so on can be analysed.

All these areas have the great advantage for teachers that they can capitalise on areas of close and *topical* concern for their students. The risk which such an approach carries, of course, is that the teacher may be seen as 'trespassing' on the personal interests of pupils, which they had previously been able to keep rigidly separated from their school work.

Institutions

Two other concepts are analysed in media studies for GCSE – Institutions and Representation. Institutions has always seemed the most problematic area to teach in that it can be difficult to obtain sufficient reliable up-to-date information about the nature of media institutions, especially at a time like the present when new institutions – satellite broadcasting etc – are constantly being launched and multi-national corporations control much of the media. However, media studies textbooks with recent, reliable information are starting to appear and once again the question of who is setting the agenda can be asked. Is it right that so much power should be concentrated in the hands of a relatively small number of corporations – News International, Pearsons, etc?

On a more practical level, students can arrange – or, rather, their teachers can arrange – visits to record companies, newspaper offices etc or ask representatives of such institutions to visit them. Students can take the roles of media professionals and hold editorial conferences, plan advertising campaigns for imaginary products, practise the 'scheduling game' in which to put together a world-beating programme for early evening television. The subject area of Institutions, which includes 'alternative' institutions such as pirate radios and 'fanzines' etc, covers all these areas and many others.

Representation

Representation as a subject area looks at the way in which ideas, individuals and groups are represented in the media. It examines the concept of the 'star': What makes a media star? How are stars promoted and marketed? It asks how often and in what context certain groups such as racial minorities or the elderly are seen in the media. Equally important, how often are such groups *not* seen, invisible to the mass media, and what conclusions can be drawn from their absence? Once again the question of 'Who sets the agenda?' makes us ask whether the agenda deliberately excludes certain groups. Are the media simply 'windows on the world' as their proponents sometimes suggest, or is there a case to be answered that only certain socially-approved values and subjects are represented?

I hope these comments have sketched a brief picture of the current status and nature of media studies as a GCSE subject. I would now like to look briefly at the questions facing media studies at the present time and tentatively suggest some possible ways forward in the subject and related areas of the curriculum in secondary schools.

The future

There are at present three ways in which media studies might develop in schools. The first is as a separate subject. The introduction of GCSE gave media studies a status which it lacked when it was taken only at CSE level, and the increasing introduction of 'A' level media studies syllabuses can only enhance that status. However, the introduction of the National Curriculum may lead to pressure on minority subjects and a consequent 'squeeze' on media studies. One solution could lie in teachers pressing for additional status for the subject, including the introduction of media studies departments, especially as otherwise many media teachers, being primarily teachers of English, history etc, may be promoted out of the subject or leave a particular school without being replaced. The likelihood is that media studies will remain, for the forseeable future, a subject with a growing but still a minority appeal.

A second possibility is for media studies as a separate subject being extended or replaced by the concept of 'Media education across the curriculum', in other words making all teachers in a school responsible for media education within their subject. The parallel with 'language across the curriculum', the initiative which sprang from the Bullock Report in the 1970s, is not an encouraging one. The danger with every teacher becoming responsible for 'media education' is that no-one will feel responsible for the detailed study of the media and the concept, after an initial burst of enthusiasm, will evaporate. Consequently, I have little faith in the potential of this initiative.

Third, there is the idea that the media can be taught through specific, related subjects, in particular, English and technology. A clear link exists with technology in the focus on practical media productions; however, media studies teachers have been traditionally suspicious of this link on 'technicist' grounds, ie that an absorption in practice at the expense of theory will be to the overall detriment of the approach.

The link with English is stronger but also more problematic.

The recent Cox Report (*English 11-16 in the National Curriculum*) came out with a strong emphasis on the importance of media education, thanks largely to the contribution made by the British Film Institute. However, there are shifts of emphasis in the report – at one stage it emphasises the importance of reading at the expense of 'other *more passive* forms of entertainment', ie the media. There are traces, here, of the Leavisite approach of stressing rigour in dealing with literature, partly in order that the student can be 'defended' against the 'onslaught' of the mass media.

Such an approach does not bode well for a possible combined 'English and media education' approach which would, in any case, necessitate the re-writing of present GCSE English syllabuses (although at least one English 'mature' syllabus contains a media studies unit). One possible answer might be to introduce a dual certification of English and media studies syllabuses or to make the point to teachers that dual certification of English and English Literature syllabuses has freed the timetable for the introduction of media studies in place of the traditional spot that was occupied by a separate English Literature course.

I should like to conclude this brief survey of the present state of media studies teaching with a few comments of my own on the subject. Although I am a subject officer for media studies and hence have a vested interest in its survival as a separate subject, I am not entirely convinced that it could not be absorbed under the overall umbrella of English. The principal advantage of the conceptually-based subject I have described is that it provides a unified theoretical rather than content-led approach; the principal disadvantage is that some of the distinctions drawn may be seen as giving a spurious authority to essentially trivial phenomena of our time such as soap operas.

Three other dangers concern me. First, many media studies teachers seem to see themselves as engaged in a campaign to win hearts and minds, rather than simply to teach their subject. They ask 'Who is setting the agenda?' suggesting that it is a right-wing agenda which is being set, without appearing to appreciate that they may be setting a far more rigid left-wing orthodoxy in its place. Second, they may be using the authority of a media studies course to teach what interests them as film-enthusiasts, comic-enthusiasts etc. There is, again, nothing necessarily wrong with this approach, provided that they are aware of what they are doing and capable of being dispassionate about it. Third, and last, the subject depends far too much at present on the use of specialised jargon; greater use of plain English is required.

Media studies has made remarkable progress over the past twenty years in schools and the future continues to look bright for its expansion. I remain confident about its survival both as a separate subject and as a subject area within English. I also consider that it is vitally important, for the sake of students' understanding of the complex world in which we live, that the future of media education in schools should not be sacrificed on the altar of educational dogma.

17 Newspapers in education

Richard Beamish

The local newspaper stands out as an obvious classroom resource, well used by many experienced educational practitioners. It is cost-effective (particularly when supplied at discount or free by the publisher), up-to-date, related to the pupils' own environment and treats the reader as an adult. It is a window to the real world and considers the important local issues of the day. As most newspapers are full of variety, most readers will find something of interest.

The main difficulty that one tends to encounter with teachers who have not previously used newspapers as a resource is in providing adequate starting points – enabling individuals to use a live resource as and when appropriate to their and their pupils' needs. Most can conceive of the use of such material within specific media studies courses but may be a little more doubtful of its general use – contributing to media education in a cross-curricular context. Hence the use of the workshop situation, which enables teachers, teacher advisers and others to sample some of the uses to which newspapers can be put for themselves. They also have the opportunity to share experiences together and to have time to consider related issues such as the implications of the National Curriculum for this kind of work. A typical workshop for around 20 teachers (preferably from all four Key Stages) would contain the following kinds of activity:

Initial activity (all) – how to be an ace reporter

Explain the basic questions that every good reporter will ask – WHO?, WHAT?, WHERE?, WHEN?, WHY? and HOW?.

Display on an overhead projector transparency.

Give out a set of newspapers to participants (often courtesy of the local publisher) to verify that these questions have been answered in most news stories. It is best to use the same day's paper where possible, still bound to eliminate the possibility of choosing only those stories that fit.

Introduce the 'Inverse Pyramid' concept for writing a news story (see figure 17.1 overleaf, which can be used as an OHP transparency and/or as a handout). Essentially:

Headline – Summary and/or angle on story to catch the reader's attention

1st paragraph – Tells the whole story, often with an angle. Often contains only one sentence and usually less than 30 words.

2nd paragraph – Provides the most important detail to support the story.

3rd paragraph – Provides important detail to support the story.

———

———

Last paragraph – least important detail, although still relevant to the story.

Participants may well wish to speculate as to why news stories are almost always written in this way (grasp and hold the reader's attention early, paragraphs can be deleted from the bottom up without affecting the sense of the story etc).

Then comes the participants' turn. Provide them with a story. This could be on video, acted or simply told didactically. If practical, make it vaguely amusing with the possibility of using puns in the headline. You might wish to include some traps, eg, mention a high court judge without referring to the judge's gender. Your 'reporters' will almost certainly refer to the judge as male.

The participants' task is to write a headline, first, second and last paragraph of a news story on the above event. A time limit of ten minutes is not sufficient to allow them to finish but will provide a taste of what the activity involves. You could throw in a catch at the last minute – half the group writes as though they are working for the local paper while the other half is writing for the *Sun*!

Compare some examples. This is usually quite amusing and gives rise to a number of discussion points. In debate, consider the implications of this kind of exercise for classroom activity. Does it

Figure 17.1

The Inverse Pyramid

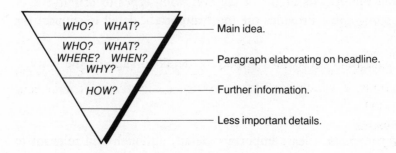

WHO?   WHAT? ———————— Main idea.

WHO?   WHAT?
WHERE?   WHEN? ———————— Paragraph elaborating on headline.
WHY?

HOW? ———————— Further information.

———————— Less important details.

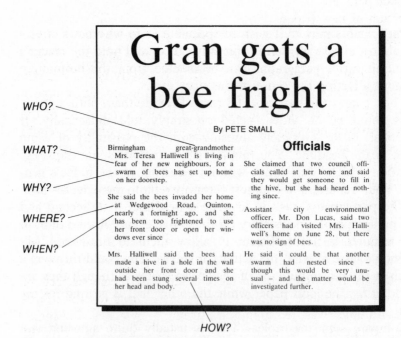

Gran gets a
bee fright

By PETE SMALL

WHO?

WHAT?

WHY?

WHERE?

WHEN?

Birmingham great-grandmother Mrs. Teresa Halliwell is living in fear of her new neighbours, for a swarm of bees has set up home on her doorstep.

She said the bees invaded her home at Wedgewood Road, Quinton, nearly a fortnight ago, and she has been too frightened to use her front door or open her windows ever since

Mrs. Halliwell said the bees had made a hive in a hole in the wall outside her front door and she had been stung several times on her head and body.

Officials

She claimed that two council officials called at her home and said they would get someone to fill in the hive, but she had heard nothing since.

Assistant city environmental officer, Mr. Don Lucas, said two officers had visited Mrs. Halliwell's home on June 28, but there was no sign of bees.

He said it could be that another swarm had nested since – though this would be very unusual – and the matter would be investigated further.

HOW?

encourage reading, writing, speaking and listening? How does it fit within the National Curriculum Attainment Targets?

Examples of similar work developed by practising teachers can also be distributed that specifically encourage reading activities, and writing in a particular style and for a specific target audience.

Group work

Group work can follow the above type of exercise. Included among the options might be the following types of activity:

Project work

Intention:
To enable teachers to discover the wide range of educational situations to which regional newspapers can make a useful contribution.

Equipment:
Card
Marker pens etc
Selection of newspapers

Method:
Newspapers, communications and the media are all popular headings for cross-curricular project work, particularly in the primary phase but also in a team teaching context in the secondary phase.

Your task is to construct a diagram that illustrates some of the ways in which newspapers (with other media if you wish) could be used as an educational resource and as a source of study in themselves, within such a topic.

Looking at some of the papers available may help to get you started. For instance, is there anything of interest in the advertisements – maths or the study of persuasion, for example?

You may use the large sheets of paper and marker pens for the diagram(s).

If you have time, consider in more detail how specific aspects of such a project might be put into action in terms of educational aims and objectives, teaching and learning approaches, and monitoring progress. You may even wish to address the area of primary/secondary transition. On the other hand, you might not!

Every picture tells a story

Intention:
To better understand the advantages and limitations of non-verbal communication, particularly with regard to the interpretation of a pre-determined fixed image.

Equipment:
Photographs selected at random from newspapers OR reject glossy photographs obtained from a newspaper office
Large sheets of paper
Scissors, paste etc.

Method:
From the newspaper photographs available to you, select one and glue it to the centre of a large sheet of paper.

1   Each group member to invent a caption for the picture and to write it underneath. As a group, select that which seems most appropriate and circle it for identification purposes.

2   Select a second picture, again glue it to a large sheet of paper and try to add comments (with arrows) on various aspects of what you see. You may crop the picture if you wish.

   This is a more creative approach than (1), but allows for an individualised interpretation of parts rather than a whole image.

   You might wish to add voice balloons to the picture in the style of *Private Eye* or even to write a mini-poem based on the topic.

3   What have you learned from this type of work?

Simulations

Intention:
To enable teachers to appreciate the wide range of educational benefits to be gained from a class or group production of a newspaper, whether for sale or as a class exercise.

Equipment:
Newspapers
Paste-up cards (available from local newspaper)
Scissors, paste etc

Word processor or desk top publishing system (not essential)
Camera(s) (not essential)

Method:
As with many other types of simulation exercise, producing a school newspaper or front page can result in all sorts of learning experiences. Children have the opportunity to write for a specific audience, whether real or imaginary, and practice many skills on the way. Reading, writing, talking and listening are all essential parts of this kind of work – much of it necessarily in Standard English. In addition, many other concepts are involved – learning to work together under time pressures, design etc.

Many newspaper simulations now use desk-top publishing systems or word processors to produce the finished article. Using such systems no longer requires any technical or programming knowledge and the time when the new technologies become an integral part of whole school curriculum delivery is fast approaching.

One of the problems often encountered with the use of microcomputers and PCs in newspaper simulations is that too much emphasis is placed on using the equipment and not enough on producing the stories, artwork etc. Your Head of Information Technology/Computer Studies, etc, will be able to advise you on the facilities available to you in your school.

This exercise is more concerned with the way in which a news story is written and how it is laid out. You will already have had a go at a news story in the first plenary session but now you will also need to plan a page.

Using the paste-up cards provided, give your front page a title and a mast-head. The best way to do this is to produce it on a sheet of plain paper, cut it to size and paste into place.

Members of the group should write brief news stories based on real incidents that have taken place at their schools (or elsewhere) in the last week. They should be written in the format suggested earlier today. The stories should be written in columns for pasting into place on the page.

There are all sorts of logistical issues to be considered. Do you need a brief editorial conference at the outset to consider which stories should go where? Do you want to include a feature or an interview? How about advertisements?

The only way to get this work even nearly complete on time is to think in terms of some division of labour. The important thing, though, is the process rather than the result. Once the principals have been grasped, the technology becomes much easier!

The object of the exercise is to get as close as possible to producing a finished page.

What are the educational implications of this kind of exercise (other than those already stated)?

Emotive language and influence

Intention:
To investigate the purposes of using emotive language.
To illustrate that local newspapers have a responsible role to play in media education

Equipment:
Selection of local newspapers
Pens, paper etc

Method:
Find an editorial from one of the newspapers available.

Do you agree with it? How would you improve it?

Attached are two extreme examples of emotive writing – adapted from popular national papers.

1   Having read the articles, try and write a leader (editorial) of 150 words, expressing your views on schools having the right to opt out of the State system, Prince Charles' views on the teaching of English, or some other contentious topic. Try to make a reasoned argument.

2   Try to re-write the article, adding emotive language where possible.

3   As a group, discuss your responses and consider whether the use of emotive language in this context makes it more interesting to read. Does it distort the issues or seek to persuade unfairly?

Interviews

Intention:
To gain an insight into the effectiveness of our oral communication, often coloured by the receiver's perceptions.

To gain an understanding of the interviewing process and the way in which information thus gained is translated into an article.

Equipment:
Selection of local newspapers
Room layout to facilitate working in pairs
Pens, paper etc

Method:
1 Find a feature article that comprises an interview and consider how it is structured.
2 Working in pairs, interview your partner about his/her life, leading up to the reasons for attendance here today. Try to find an angle that will interest the reader. Take such notes as are necessary.
3 Change roles.
4 Write a 150 word article about your partner and add a head-line.
5 As a group, compare notes. Have you used a different style from the way news stories are written? Did you find an angle?
6 What are the implications of this kind of work for children's talking, listening, writing and reading?

Concluding activities

Depending on the time available, two further activities can be utilised to bring the INSET session to a productive conclusion. The first is to operate a further group session in which participants are asked to think of ways in which they might wish to use newspapers in their daily teaching and as part of a cross-curricular/cross-phase project. Methodologies for this vary but the net result is that individuals have had to think in terms of ap-plying the ideas considered during the day to their own classroom, to their own style of teaching and to the needs of their pupils, all within the constraints of the National Curriculum Attainment Targets and Schemes of Work, where these are known. Towards the end of this session, participants could also be asked to note down any questions, comments or reservations that they might have concerning this type of activity.

The above work can then lead into a report back session and a

'Question Time' exercise. In the latter, some of the written points from the previous session are put to a panel of 'experts', comprising the course leader, a local newspaper representative and such others as may be appropriate. It is important, of course, for the Chairperson to wear a cardboard bow-tie!

Finally, a brief discussion on 'Where now?' would effectively close the day. As with all INSET activity, follow-up and monitoring are all important if the optimum benefit is to be derived.

No time limits have been placed on the various components of a day such as this because amounts of time available for such sessions can vary so much. They are documented here merely to indicate the *kind* of work that can take place.

Teacher workshops such as these have been an important factor in helping to establish Newspapers in Education schemes in various parts of the country. At the time of writing, there are at least 65 publishers working with local schools, usually in conjunction with the local education authority. It is viewed very much as a partnership; teachers are able to bring the real world into the classroom, encourage both basic and higher order reading skills, and enable a critical appreciation of the media. For its part, the local newspaper is enabling young people, tomorrow's readers, to see what services their products provide, albeit warts and all.

Some Newspapers in Education schemes involve seconded teachers and some full-time employees, but the majority are smaller scale activities. There are sometimes links with such groups as the Technical and Vocational Education Initiative or the School Curriculum and Industry Project, while in other situations liaison is through an interested adviser and/or the local professional development centre. In all such situations, the result has been a greater interest in what local newspapers have to offer, whether through children's work appearing in print in-paper, through newspaper simulations given real meaning through local paper support or through the general use of a live and current resource.

Participating teachers have also produced a series of teaching materials that have been published by the Newspaper Society, and this approach is set to continue with a new series of teaching ideas related to the National Curriculum being devised and trialled by practising teachers.

For further information on Newspapers in Education and a contact name at your local newspaper (where practical), contact:

Richard Beamish
Manager: Newspapers in Education
The Newspaper Society
74–77 Great Russell Street
London
WC1B 7DB
Tel: 071 636 7014

18 The language of advertising

Norma Mudd

Introduction

For some time now reading researchers have been urging teachers to prepare children far more adequately for the ever-increasing demands of today's society in terms of literacy. However, it seems that some teachers still view reading in the narrow context of what may be termed as 'school reading'. Martin and Merritt (1989) refer to the mismatch between the reading demands of school and those of everyday life. Moreover, Moyle (1982) refers to adults who may 'have only a limited range of strategies when it comes to *using* language' (my italics).

It seems that the language of advertising could provide an ideal starting point from which to prepare our children to become effectively literate adults and effective users of language. Advertising exposes the public to bias and propaganda; it may attack overtly or it may penetrate our subconscious quite insidiously. It can also provide children with a wide range of language which is 'dictated' by the authors' aims and audiences (such provision being further recommendations made by Kingman and Cox).

Although many people understand advertising to mean manufacturers talking to their customers, we should remember that advertising is basically a form of communication and may vary from government notices persuading drivers to wear seat belts or informing the public about rent rebates to employers recruiting staff or the manufacturers of a breakfast cereal persuading us to buy their particular breakfast cereal because it is fun to eat.

Effective advertising generally contains carefully constructed language, often combined with graphic illustrations in which shape and colour may play important roles in persuading a target audience to take notice of the information communicated. It seems that we may help children to become more effective readers and users of language in today's society if we help them to become aware of such advertisers' ploys as they seek to persuade by informing, amusing, shocking, misleading etc. We may alert children also to what advertisers may *not* tell us, as is exemplified in particular by estate and travel agents. Moreover, teachers may take this opportunity of discussing with the children what *specific* features of oral and written language make it appropriate for different occasions according to speakers' or authors' aims.

Since we learn best by experience, it seems that one of the best ways of alerting children to some of the wide range of advertising ploys is to encourage them to become advertisers themselves, communicating various messages to the public in appropriate language, and using effective advertising techniques. Moreover, whilst teachers are encouraging children to use their oral and written language selectively, it seems that it is an ideal opportunity to help them to understand some of the technical terms of their language. As Brinton and Palmer (1988, p 78) observe about language (and grammar) '. . . the more we know about it, the more we understand it, the better we will be able to control our use of it.' Similarly, Kingman and Cox (1988) advocate that children should know more about the technical terms used to describe language (though apart from stating that it should be introduced 'naturally' they do not explain *how* such knowledge should be imparted). Of course, there are many ways of using the language of advertising as a starting point for preparing children to become effective and actively literate adults. This article, however, will describe just one method which was used with a group of thirty children aged between nine and eleven years during six teaching sessions. Each session lasted just over one hour. The work produced by the children subsequent to the 'training' sessions will also be described briefly and an informal evaluation of their experiences will be made.

Different language for different occasions

Since most children tend to adjust their oral language in particular according to purpose and audience (see MacLean and Chapman, 1989) this was made a starting point for class discussion. The children gave many examples of when changes occur in register in their oral language. Examples included the difference in tone and vocabulary used to persuade adults to let them stay up late compared with the tone and vocabulary used to indicate disagreement with some decision made by a peer. After approximately fifteen minutes of discussion on this topic, it seemed appropriate to let the children try out some practical 'explorations' in using language according to audience and purpose. Thus, the thirty children were divided into ten groups; each group of three children was given a card containing written instructions regarding some form of communication to be carried out by each group member in turn. The communication on the cards did not necessarily fall into the 'advertising' category since the purpose here was simply to increase the children's sensitivity to variations in language according to audience and purpose. Listed below are four examples of the instructions written on the cards:

1   Pretend the other two members of your group are *adult* smokers. Try to persuade them to give up smoking.
2   Two new members of your class speak no English. Try to persuade them not to throw their litter on the floor.
3   Tell the other two group members about a real or imaginary frightening experience.
4   Pretend the other two members of your group are teachers. Try to persuade them to order your favourite book(s) for the school library. (You are a pupil.)

The ten groups were given approximately ten minutes in which to carry out the instructions on their cards. They then came together as a class, and each group nominated one person to represent their interpretation of the instructions. The class was invited to comment on each group's 'performance', making specific reference to the type of language used and its appropriateness. As the children spoke, I made notes on the blackboard summarising their comments on each group's work.

Comments included reference to the polite tone and the repetition of emotive phrases by a girl dissuading adults from smoking. For example: please stop wasting your money; damaging your health; killing yourself. The children considered what they called 'sign language' to be effective as used by a boy in the 'anti-litter' group. They referred to his repeated head-shaking as he pointed to the litter on the floor and also his head-nodding as he placed the litter in a waste-bin. (I introduced the children to the term 'non-verbal language' and many of them soon began using the term quite freely.)

They observed that the boy who related a frightening experience spoiled his beginning by smiling (probably he was nervous); it was also noted that he gradually adapted his tone to suit his subject. The class recalled emotive (and repeated) adjectives and nouns, for example: dark night; howling wind; loud knocking; weird cries.

It seems worth noting too that again I used the technical terms when discussing the preceding words with the children. Though some children appeared to have some knowledge of these terms, I realised that others were confusing them. Confusion seemed to be reduced when I suggested that they 'tested' common nouns (called naming words by many children) by preceding them with 'the' (the wind, the knocking ...). Similarly adjectives could be 'tested' by preceding them with 'it is' (it is dark, it is loud, it is weird ...).

Having considered some of the different ways in which we use language, verbal and non-verbal, it seemed appropriate to spend a little time discussing some of the main influences of other languages upon ours in readiness for the children's introduction to various types of advertising by the media. The following two paragraphs summarise the main information given to the children.

Our languages

We speak of our language as English, yet it would be more precise to speak of our *languages*. Modern English has two main strands, one with Saxon or Old English roots used to describe our ordinary, everyday world. For example: love; home; welcome; good. The other strand has Latinate or Old French roots; the former being used particularly with reference to the church and government; the latter (which for some time after the landing of William of Normandy in 1066 was used by the ruling classes to signify power and authority) is used with particular reference to royalty and the law.

English literature is generally considered to be trilingual, a mixture of English, Latin and French, the latter two being considered the language of romance. It is not surprising therefore, that much of the language of advertising is dominated by short, simple words which have their roots in Old English, the intention generally being to obtain immediate understanding in language which is familiar. Conversely, when, for example, advertisers seek to convince us of their technical expertise in the manufacture of a product, then words tend to be Latinate, French or Greek in origin. Thus, the manufacturers of 'Electrolux' refer to their 'versatile telescopic extension' and scent manufacturers may refer to 'an exquisite, provocative perfume' (rather than a 'lovely arousing smell').

Note This information regarding our language has been very much condensed and over-simplified. Of course our language is a complex mixture of *many* languages, and had time permitted I should have liked to discuss with the children the ever-increasing use of American and (more recently) Australian expressions in our language. Slang is a further aspect of language development which the children may have found interesting. Moreover, teachers may find that fascinating and relevant discussions on language arise if they teach in a multi-cultural school and take examples from their pupils' first languages.

The regular use of etymological dictionaries may help students of all ages to become sensitive to the influences of other languages upon our own language.

Advertisements from magazines/newspapers

Five advertisements were chosen for their varied aims, tones and use of language. They were studied first in two's and then by the class as a whole. Each child was given a folder in which to keep their individual comments.

The first advertisement studied simply showed a training shoe with its make stated boldly above it and its merits listed below. The children suggested that the audience would be anyone interested in training, jogging and keeping fit who wanted comfortable shoes which would wear well. (*Some* children thus felt that the advertisement might not apply to people over the age of thirty years!) Comments were made upon the advertiser's use of adjectives like: finest, good, real, natural, comfortable. These words were quickly categorised as being Old English in origin.

Contrasted with this, a second, and relatively sophisticated advertisement in terms of approach, was studied. It was actually promoting Nescafé sales, but attracted the potential buyer firstly by its bold headlines:

FREE! Nescafé Frappé iced coffee shaker!

Interestingly, though some children correctly identified the objective of the advertisers, others thought that coffee shakers were being sold; it does seem that some children need help in identifying misleading or ambiguous information. (It is worth noting, however, that a boy and girl working together stated in their personal notes: 'Free is an eye-catching word it makes the buyer think it's free but it's not really – it's a rip-off.')

There was initial agreement that the target audience would be mainly *women* – though, after some discussion, it was decided that the audience could be any sex and any age. The children further commented that 'Nescafé Frappé' would probably appeal to younger people, but that older people would actually *buy* the Nescafé. 'Café' and 'frappé' were quickly identified as being French words (most children knew 'café' meant 'coffee' and one boy knew that 'frappé' meant 'iced'). Several groups spotted the play on words and sound in the advertisement's exhortation to 'Have an iced day ...' All the children knew that this expression originated in the United States.

In stark contrast to the preceding advertisement, the third advertisement was promoted by Action Aid. It showed the face of an Ethiopian child; across its face the words 'Bread and Cabbage' was written five times. Most children noted the repetition and also the implications of the words. Also remarked upon was the play on the words in the stark message:

IN ETHIOPIA
ONE CHILD IN FOUR IS
DYING FOR CHANGE

Many of the children had noted in their personal folders the dramatic change in tone in this advertisement compared with the humorous, chatty language of the previous one. Many children also noted the nature of emotive words like: tragic; poverty; stricken; die; dying. They commented too on the repetition of the letter 'd' in: '... a dull diet is also a deadly diet'. (I explained that the repetition of letters or sounds is referred to as 'alliteration' and generally gives emphasis and/or rhythm to language.) There was agreement that the advertisement aimed to 'tug on your heart' (as one group said) in order to persuade people to sponsor an Ethiopian child. They felt, however, that the audience would not be poor people as the minimum donation suggested was £5.

The final two advertisements used were studied simultaneously; both publicised the use of 'All Clear', an anti-dandruff shampoo. However, one had been produced two or more years ago (referred to as A) and the other was produced in 1989 (B). The children quickly noted that A was dominated by the side view of the head of a young male, whereas B showed two side-views of heads, one male, one female. Many realised that B was therefore aimed at a wider audience. They felt that the visual images would attract mainly teenagers and people in their early twenties. They considered the tone of A to be quite chatty and identified emotive adjectives like: new; effective; clear; tough; shiny; manageable. Also, many children noted the play on words, '. . . makes you a clear promise', and 'you'll have the worry of dandruff off your shoulders.' Interestingly, they commented on the following sentence in A : 'It contains piroctol the most effective anti-dandruff agent there is' and identified 'piroctol' as being possibly Latinate since it was unfamiliar. (We tried to discover what 'piroctol' was but were unsuccessful.) Several children noted that B replaced this sentence with: 'It has extracts of herbs and leaves your hair soft. . . .' One boy commented that the altered word choice seemed to fit in with the public's growing concern for natural products. A girl pointed out that the phrase 'herbs and leaves' was misleading since 'leaves' sounded like a noun but was really a verb. (I have to confess that *I* had not spotted the ambiguity.)

Advertisements from television

Three brief television advertisements, publicising various products, were shown to the children followed by one longer television item (shown on 'Wogan') in which a choir of children appealed to the public to 'Think of the Trees'. The children noted that the former three advertisements relied greatly on humour (both visually and in the form of puns) for their impact. By now the children were becoming used to analysing the language of advertising and they commented, for example, on the alliteration of 'fastidious feline friends' and its combination of Latinate and Old English vocabulary. (Interestingly, though none of the children knew the meaning of 'fastidious' they all guessed that it was Latinate in origin.) After viewing the latter advertisement, the children noted that the visual effect of being shown healthy trees followed by a sequence of camera shots showing scenes of devastation in what had once been a forest was immediate and shocking. They observed too that the use of young and healthy children singing would gain wide audience interest, moreover, the key words in their song (for example: think; trees; living; strong; grow) were all easily understandable and so the message was clear. The use of 'catchy' music and/or sound was thought to keep the 'message' in the public's subconscious for some time.

Of significance too was the fact that, by now, many children had begun to collect a wide range of advertisements of their own. Also, many were watching television advertisements with a critical eye. Indeed, some of the most interesting discussions resulted from *their* 'findings'.

The children's advertisements

The children then began to plan their own advertisements; they could work alone or in small groups on any type of advertising, and it was interesting to note that three quarters of their advertisements related to health or environmental issues. Time (and space) do not permit a comprehensive description of their work; however, the following examples may give a representative view of the range of thought and language use that went into the children's work.

Two children worked on a brief radio script set in the year 2010 to illustrate the possibility that whales may become extinct if we do not stop their slaughter. One child spoke as herself, and the other spoke as her grandmother so that a wide audience would be reached. They emphasised man's greed and the harmless (to man) nature of the whale.

A group of five children worked on anti-smoking advertisements. Emotive words included: wasting money; murder; kill; premature birth. A packet of unnamed cigarettes with human legs and the words 'I KILL' emerging in a balloon from the packet's opening was particularly menacing. One member of the group wrote a 'poem' against smoking; later it was decided to present the poem as a rap. All the group joined in performing the rap which is shown below and which the children taped.

Smoking is Bad
Many people die every year from smoking
Are you going to be one of them?
Don't murder yourself and your children
Please Don't Smoke!
They cost a lot of dosh and
They do so much harm
Why bother with them?
They're better long gone.
Please Don't Smoke!

(The author thought that 'dosh' would be easily understood by younger smokers.)

Of course, it could be argued that a rap is not an appropriate medium, in terms of tone, for dissuading smoking. Yet the fact that many of the other children in the class soon knew the rap by heart is surely a tribute to the power/influence of music and rhythm in advertising.

The *Think of the Trees* song on television stimulated an advertisement along similar lines. In an illustration of an enlarged leaf, the children depicted one half showing thriving plants and trees and the other showing desolate wasteland. This was accompanied by simple, emotive words like: Save our trees: Now our children's children's children will have something to look forward to.

Several groups used alliteration in their advertisements. For example: Leaded is Lethal; Come to our Fabulous, Family Feast! Repetition of the key words of advertisements was very common and two boys made their repetition blatant:

Lead = Danger   Lead = Danger
Lead = Danger   Lead = Danger
Lead = Danger   Lead = Danger

And, as previously stated, there were many more advertisements prepared by the children which evidenced thoughtful use of language.

Concluding comments

As most teachers will know, though these 'end products' were important to the children, the most important aspects of this work occurred in the sessions *prior* to the completion of the final products.

During the study of the language of advertising, the children's experiences included:

- Group interaction/co-operation/decision-making;
- Following written instructions;
- Using oral and non-verbal communication according to audience and purpose;
- Evaluating and analysing the oral and non-verbal communication of peers;
- Reading (including the small print) and discussing a range of texts which were relevant to everyday life, and varied in tone and language according to author purpose and intended audience;
- Developing a critical awareness of some common advertising ploys (for example, emotive language, repetition of the main message, misleading/ambiguous information, humour, shock tactics, the use of graphics, music, etc);
- Awareness and use of some of the technical terms of our language (for example, nouns, adjectives, verbs, exclamation marks, contractions);
- Planning and re-drafting advertisements designed with a specific purpose and audience in mind;
- Using tape-recorders and making judgements about their own oral language (including features such as clarity, tone, speed and appropriateness).

All these experiences (and I am sure that many more could have been included) would seem to be the beginnings of preparing our children to become not only critical, effective readers and users of language, but also caring members of society, capable of working and talking together to achieve common goals.

References

Brinton, P. and Palmer, S. (1988) Bring back grammar (or 'meta-linguistics' if you must). In Anderson, C. (ed) *Reading: the ABC and beyond*. London: Macmillan, for UKRA.

DES (March, 1988) Report of the Committee of Inquiry into the Teaching of English Language (The Kingman Report). London: HMSO.

—— (November, 1988) *English for ages 5 to 11*. Proposals of the Secretary of State for Education and Science and the Secretary of State for Wales (The Cox Report). London: National Curriculum Council.

Maclean, M. and Chapman, L. J. (1989) The processing of cohesion in fiction and non fiction by good and poor readers. In *Journal of Research in Reading*. Oxford: Blackwell, for UKRA.

Martin, T. and Merritt, J. (1989) Text comprehension and study skills. In M. Hunter-Carsch (ed) *The art of reading*. Oxford: Blackwell, for UKRA.

Moyle, D. (1982) *Children's words*. London: Grant McIntyre.

Acknowledgements

I should like to thank Lesley Duckworth (Headteacher) and all the staff at Burscough County Primary School for their kindness and co-operation during this work on advertising.

19 Writers and readers: what do they know? An analysis of six stories written by and for children

Ann Browne

The work of Ferreiro and Teberosky (1983), Hall (1987), Newman (1984) and Smith (1983), has drawn attention to children's early literacy knowledge and understanding of the communicative function of writing. It has also demonstrated children's ability to communicate through writing and drawing at an early age. Given that one accepts children's understanding and ability before school, what do children learn about written forms once they become literate? What do they learn about the way that written language and illustrations work in books and stories and how might they demonstrate this knowledge in their own writing?

What follows is an analysis of some written work undertaken during a project in which eight-year-old children were asked to write and illustrate a book for a five-year-old partner who was a beginning reader.

The project

Six five-year-old children in their first term at school, identified as being at the very beginning stages of reading, were selected as recipients of the books to be written. The criteria for the selection of these particular children included their apparent need for motivation and enhanced self-esteem and being likely to benefit from involvement in a project that would enable them to see themselves as readers. They did not appear to have a great deal of knowledge about print and were not at the stage of independent reading, even of the simplest texts.

The six authors were volunteers from a class of eight-year-old children who wished to participate in the project as part of their class topic on books. Their abilities in reading and writing, as assessed by the class teacher, varied from very competent (Robert) to poor (Jonathan). The nature of the project was explained to both groups of children. At the first meeting of all twelve children the subject matter for the books was named by the five-year-olds. The older children then chose the topic they would write a book about and consequently chose their partner and particular audience. This project was based on an idea suggested by Baum (1985).

The choice of subject matter and partners

The five-year-old children had been asked to think about books and told that they were going to have a book written especially for them on a subject or about a character of their choice. The items chosen revealed something of what this group of five-year-olds thought was an appropriate topic for a book.

Recipient		*Writer*
Daniel	Miss Muffet	Jonathan
Sarah	Little Bo-Peep	Eleanor
Mark	Thomas the Tank Engine	Hew
Louise	About a dog	Robert
Tamsin	About a kitten	Emma
Robin	Postman Pat	Ben

It is interesting that their choices were influenced by TV programmes and associated books, nursery rhymes, and common central characters in early reading books: a dog and a kitten. This group of children seemed to have already learned about typical genres and characters that they might expect to appear in reading material for their age range. None chose a real life central character eg a boy or girl. None chose a situation, perhaps indicating that it is characters who are central to children's enjoyment of books and, in any case, the character may partly define the situation. It was the eight-year-olds' choice of character that decided the pairings of the children and, apart from Louise and Robert, all pairings were between children of the same sex. With such a small sample of children it is difficult to tell whether Postman Pat and Thomas the Tank Engine are in the main more appealing to boys than kittens and Little Bo Peep. Applebee (1978) suggests that in story books dogs are associated with male readers and characters, and cats with female readers and characters. Robert, the second to last child to choose from the list of characters, had the choice of kitten or dog and his choice may reflect Applebee's findings. Robert showed no dislike of having a girl for a partner but his story was the poorest in both written form and illustration. As he had been identified as the most able child in the group, this was at first surprising. It might be explained by the pairing or the fact that he found this task difficult because he was used to writing creatively for himself and for his teacher, rather than a defined audience, or perhaps he was not stimulated by the topic. Louise had specifically asked that the story be set in Skiathos where she had spent her holidays. The lack of knowledge about this setting may have made the task more offputting. When asked about his story Robert offered no clues as to his feelings about the task. Louise was the only child disappointed with her book. This disappointment was associated with the lack of a 'real' story.

The stories

Three of the six stories are reproduced here in their entirety, ie text and illustrations. The three selected show the greatest variety of story and illustrative features and the influence of societal norms and values. The stories are reproduced as they appeared in their final version, typed, illustrated and arranged by the authors.

Miss Muffet *by Jonathan for Daniel*

This story was extended by its illustrations, showing, for example, the boy and the spider climbing a tall house not unlike a tower which might be a feature associated with children's fairy stories. Thus Jonathan set the story in place and time through his illustrations. He makes no mention of location in the text. Jonathan introduces a boy as a central character, perhaps to suit

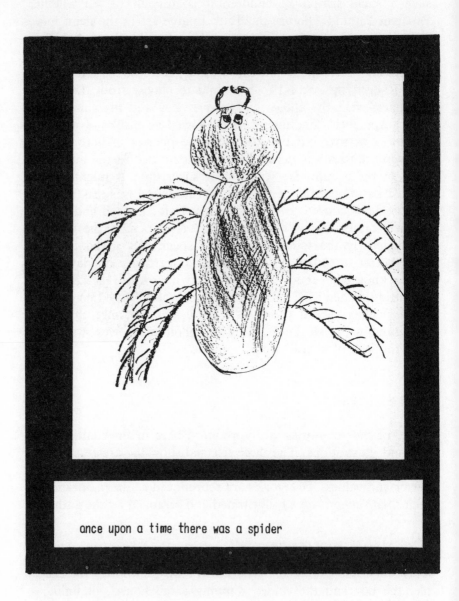

once upon a time there was a spider

and a   little boy dressed up as a robber and
he steals food

the boy and the little spider sneaked up and
the little spider and the little boy made
little miss muffet jump

she ran away and the little boy stole little
miss muffets food

his male audience and certainly giving a new twist to the original nursery rhyme. Miss Muffet, identified in the title as the central character, is marginalised both by the spider and by the boy. The boy is portrayed as an active, mischievous character, Miss Muffet as a passive character demonstrating stereotypical female behaviour. She does not appear in the text until page three.

Little Bo Peep *by Eleanor for Sarah*

Eleanor demonstrates a great deal of knowledge about stories, about writing and about readers. She uses the original nursery rhyme as a vehicle for a new story, neatly incorporating it into her version. She did this in order not to disappoint Sarah. Eleanor thought Sarah would probably like to read the original rhyme but as author she wanted to produce a more interesting story and knew that authors have the authority to change events and produce 'the proper story'. She was also determined to use book language eg 'comforted' and 'a-fleeting'. Eleanor asserted that Sarah would understand 'comforted' since it was clear in the story and accompanying illustrations that the boy was helping Bo-Peep. She was not so sure about Sarah's understanding of 'a-fleeting' and so provided an explanation of this word on the next page of her book, 'And they saw the sheep running away'. By doing this she seems to be aware of the distance between the author and the audience and that as a consequence the author needs to make written language explicit so that the reader can fully understand the author's message.

She uses humour in her writing as she changes and adds to the story. She also demonstrates a clear knowledge of the conventions of the fairy tale genre, 'they were married'. She accepts without question the notion of the passive female character in spite of her willingness to change and add to the original nursery rhyme. Another fairy tale aspect that Eleanor uses to advantage is the dream sequence. In fairy stories dreams may reflect reality or they may be a device whereby an undesirable occurrence is introduced and the solution is found when the dreamer awakes. Both of these possibilities seem to be present in Eleanor's story. The introduction of the boy character makes it possible for Eleanor to incorporate the notion of care into her story. The phrase 'they were married' fits the mood of wholeness. It seems that Eleanor feels strongly that stories should have resolutions. The original Little

There was once a little girl called little Bo-peep
now I will tell you the proper story.

little Bo-peep has lost her sheep , and doesn't
know where to find them ,
leave them alone , and they'll come home   ,
bringing their tails behind them .

little Ba-peep fell fast asleep
and dreamt she heard them bleating
but when she awoke , she found it a joke ,
for they were a-fleeting.

and little Bo–peep said
   " my sheep are lost"
so the little boy comforted her.

And they saw the sheep running away
so the little boy ran away and caught them.

so he took them all back to little Bo-peep and
they were married.

Bo-Peep nursery rhyme ends in chaos, but by breaking out of the limitations imposed by rhyme, Eleanor is able to end the story satisfactorily: the sheep are found and Bo-Peep has a permanent companion.

Thomas the Tank Engine *by Hew for Mark*

The narrative is remarkable not just for the sense of story which Hew displays by including a beginning, anticipation of disaster, the enigmatic preparation for the climax ('and you will never guess what happened next'), the climax and the resolution, but also for its overall presentation. Hew has carefully placed one sentence on each page, explained and extended by exact illustrations that both support the text and add detail. Such details as the weather and Thomas's feelings might be too complex and distracting to be written into the text but are easily incorporated into the story through the illustrations. Not only is Thomas's smiling face re-placed by a downturned mouth when he is derailed but the smoke ceases to come out of the chimney, indicating that Thomas is both sad and static. The equivalence of stillness with sadness indicates to the reader that this is not an enjoyable adventure with the possibility of an exciting consequence but an accident that necessi-tates action from an outside agent in order to restore Thomas' happiness. Although Hew's story is apparently one of the simplest of the six, it demands that the reader 'reads' both text and illustra-tion in order to both understand the plot and understand the character's feelings.

Writers and readers: what do they know?

The writers demonstrate a range and wealth of knowledge about writing and books. They are all clear about the nature of a story for young children. It has a limited number of characters includ-ing a central character, a simple plot which takes the form of action, subsequent action and a happy or satisfying resolution. Within this simple framework the action may be used to create tension, that is, something sad or unexpected happens and has to be resolved. Humour is and can be mixed with tension. Eleanor and Hew both let the reader share the author's knowledge of the outcome while demonstrating that the characters do not know

One day, Thomas was pulling the coaches

Just ahead there was a big gap

He carried on going

and you will never guess what happened next

CRASH Thomas had come off the rails

he had bumped into the Fat Controllers house

The men got him out with Gordon and some planks

what will happen next. The stories progress in a temporal sequence. The children use their awareness of book language, 'once
upon a time', 'one day', 'then', 'so' etc to move the action along.
The inclusion of such phrases and the use of the past tense as a
narrative device show that the writers have absorbed the language
and style of books for young readers. Eleanor shows by her use of
a dialogue bubble that she is aware of the differences between
spoken and written language. They all paid attention to detail in
both text and illustration and their use of language is concise,
appropriate and vivid.

The books include many of the features that aid understanding
and enjoyment of stories referred to by Geva and Olson (1983).
Such features include use of a story grammar, use of the past tense,
and use of a linear temporal structure. These children, aged eight
and acting as writers, seem to have a much more sophisticated
knowledge of how stories work than Geva and Olson's six-year-olds
engaged in a story telling exercise, although the differences between oral and written tasks must be acknowledged. Their additional time at home and at school as listeners, readers and writers
has apparently enabled them to learn a great deal about the nature
of books and stories. By using the devices that would seem to be
universal, they produced books that were accessible to younger
readers.

The nature of this particular project placed constraints upon the
writers. It gave them a particular purpose for writing and audience
to address. The choice of subject matter and audience was
limited and may not have coincided with the individual author's
interests. This group of eight-year-olds, who were used to and
able to produce long pieces of writing, had to limit their output
and make it suitable for a non-reading audience. It is possible that
the constraints of the task were helpful in encouraging the children to think more carefully about what and how they wrote and
about how they might use illustrations in their books. The children were meticulous in checking their drafts against the picture
books available in the classroom. By the end of the project they
were generally proud of their books and keen to share them with
their audience and any other child who was interested. In short
these children were able to 'experience the joys of authorship'
(Graves, 1983) and demonstrated that they had, on the whole,
taken the author's responsibility to interest and entertain the reader very seriously.

During the course of the project the writers realised the advantages of planning before writing a final draft. They recognised the need to communicate efficiently and attention was paid to conventional spelling, punctuation and to the final layout of the text when it was typed up by the children on a jumbo typewriter. They also discovered the importance of note taking when consulting with their readers. They needed little help in realising that in this project 'writing is for someone and something, that it has an audience and purpose as well as a topic' (Wallen, 1986). During the composition and on examining the finished books, the authors show what they know about the needs and expectations of young readers. It seems that they know that reading is about gaining meaning from both text and illustrations. Reading should be a pleasurable experience both fitting the reader's expectations and giving entertainment to the reader. The text needs to be simple but need not be dull and it can make demands on the reader as long as the reader is given help with those demands.

The recipients of the books also displayed competencies that might normally have been overlooked. During the consultation sessions they demonstrated that they understood the idea of a story and of a book by identifying appropriate book topics. During the reading sessions they demonstrated first that they could listen to a story following text and pictures, then join in with a story, identifying words and reading unknown words relying on context and memory. Given predictable material, material that was personally important, and prior knowledge of the text, they could approach texts with confidence expecting a story. The readers' reactions to their stories showed their critical awareness and clear expectations about books.

Conclusions

Within this project the children were able to demonstrate a range and generally high level of language competencies. What led them to compose and to guide the composition as they did? By analysing the books and the literacy behaviour of the children involved in the project one can see that the children have probably been influenced by stories they have heard, books they have read, their experience as readers, writing tasks they have previously done and comments and instructions they have received about writing and reading. From this they have extracted a degree of understanding and awareness of books and writing which must lead us as teachers to consider carefully the materials, tasks and comments that we give to children from their first days at school, since it appears that children know a great deal more than they are directly taught.

References

Applebee, A. N. (1978) *The child's concept of story*. London: University of Chicago Press.

Baum, A. (1985) Children writing for others. *Reading*, 19(1).

Ferreiro, E. & Teberosky, A. (1983) *Literacy before schooling*. London: Heinemann.

Geva, E. & Olson, D. (1983) Children's story-retelling. *First Language*, 4(11).

Graves, D. (1983) *Writing: teachers & children at work*. London: Heinemann.

Hall, N. (1987) *The emergence of literacy*. London: Hodder & Stoughton.

Newman, J. (1984) *The craft of children's writing*. London: Scholastic.

Smith, F. (1983) Learning to read by reading. In Smith, F. *Essays into literacy*. London: Heinemann Educational Books.

Wallen, M. (1986) First, find an audience. *Child Education*, November 1986.

20 Strategies for involving young children in word processing

Jane Medwell

The use of word processing in the primary school is now firmly established by the National Curriculum. The programmes of study for English state that at 7:

'pupils should be able to compose at greater length than they can manage to write down themselves ... by using a word processor. Pupils should be able to produce copies of work drafted on a computer and encouraged to incorporate the print out in other work including displays.' (DES 1989: 17.39)

At 11:

'They should have opportunities to create, polish and produce (individually or collaboratively, by hand or by computer) extended written texts, appropriately set out and illustrated, such as class newspapers, anthologies of stories or poems, guidebooks, etc' (DES, 1989: 17.41)

The Design and Technology report (DES, 1989) mentions the storage and drafting uses of word processing and also states that top juniors should be able to 'Use IT to present information in a variety of forms for a specific purpose, for example a newspaper or magazine for parents or other pupils' (p 76). This section recognises the power attached to presentation in and out of school, and seems to indicate that not only word processing but also desk top publishing is essential in our primary schools. The National Curriculum dictates that we shall use word processing but, as teachers, we need to concern ourselves with why and how we will integrate it into our practice. In this chapter I will briefly consider the 'why' of using word processing and desk top publishing, and then go on to consider a number of strategies for using them with a primary class.

To look at what is expected of children using the word processor we can return to the Cox report (DES, 1989), which includes not only the programmes of study, but the assumptions that underlie them. One of the assumptions about writing is that the child should be allowed to 'exercise more conscious and critical control over the writing process' and that there are identifiable strands of development 'which are to do with an increasing ability to:

- write in different forms for different purposes and audiences;
- write coherently about a wide range of topics, issues, ideas, incidents, etc; organising different kinds of texts in ways which help the reader;
- craft writing which is significantly different from speech ... and write in a style which is appropriate for the purpose, audience and subject matter;
- know when and how to plan, draft, redraft, revise and proof read their work;
- understand the nature and functions of written language.

(DES, 1989: 17.5)

All classrooms provide a wealth of subjects, audiences, and formats for writing but some teachers feel daunted by the idea of children 'crafting' writing through drafting; yet this is how many children come to understand the nature and function of written language. Word processing and desk top publishing have a great deal to offer in crafting writing. They do not only 'fit in' to a process approach to writing, but encourage children to become involved in the process of writing, and help them to understand it.

Word processing offers a number of advantages; the most obvious of these is probably instant success. Even young children can compose writing which looks good and therefore communicates effectively. Eventually we expect children to improve the quality of their work through drafting, revising and editing which is laborious and time consuming. The word processor uses a great deal less effort than drafting by hand as it offers unparallelled ease of editing; children can move bits of text, delete or add pieces, rearrange ideas and correct spellings within minutes. They, therefore, tend to be more willing to change their work without fear of recopying. When working on word processors children are more likely to see the point of changing their work as most of it will be 'public' in the sense that it is intended for an audience apart from the child and the teacher.

These are some of the advantages associated with word processing, but there are others which are associated with the use of desk top publishing. This is simply publishing without the typesetter; the author can arrange the text as he wants it, ready for publication. There are programs on the market, such as *Typesetter*, and *Pendown*, which offer a variety of fonts and are suitable for the upper primary age range. Children are perceptive about the features of writing in real life, and set out to emulate these. With desk top publishing they are able to produce realistic writing, and in doing so they learn to use appropriate styles and vocabulary. One of the advantages of these packages is the range of formats that can be produced. Children can write books, newspapers, guidebooks, posters, etc; and produce them in a style that suits the purpose and audience.

The electronic cut and paste facility offered by packages such as *Typesetter* allows children to arrange the text how and where they want on the page. This is important for the final appearance of the product, but it is also a valuable aid to allow children to organise text in a way that suits the reader; a task which involves looking through the reader's eyes. Whilst word processing enhances provisionality and so allows reflectiveness and precise shaping of text, for the primary teacher it also has another major benefit – it encourages co-operation. On one level this may mean collaborative writing. Real co-operation among young writers is hard to achieve, but the word processor seems to ease this. It may be that the public nature of the screen is less 'owned' than a book, or that the text is more open to experimentation, but in my experience it is an ideal start to collaborative writing.

Having discussed some of the benefits of word processing for the children's writing, I shall now discuss some of the strategies that could be used to incorporate it into classrooms.

Use of computer time

In view of the wording of the IT report (DES 1989) and the financial demands already made on schools, it seems likely that many schools will have to struggle on with their inadequate provision of one computer for a number of classes. Teachers will have to use this limited time for data handling programs, LOGO, spreadsheets, etc, as well as word processing. It is essential, therefore, that time is put to the best use to allow all children maximum possible experience. This may mean this experience is balanced across the year, rather than the week or term. One way to make the most of word processing time is to limit the type of writing that is done on the machine. It is possible that all writing would benefit from use of a computer but, alas, this is unrealistic. There are two simple criteria for choosing writing which makes best use of limited word processing facilities:

1 writing intended for an audience other than the teacher and writer;
2 collaborative writing.

Pieces that meet these criteria make the best use of the way in which word processing can encourage collaborative writing, and of the stimulus of a real audience. These are factors that encourage care in quality and format. Tasks such as books for younger children, newspapers, reports of science work, etc are suitable in that these pieces benefit most from the flexibility of rearrangement offered by the word processor.

Class introduction of programs

When using a new word processing or desk top publishing program it is useful to do a whole class session simply introducing the program. The information to be introduced will depend on the program. A set format program like *Front Page Extra* which creates a newspaper page may need a simple run through of how to put in a date, price, headline and story, whereas, with a more complicated program like *Typesetter*, it will be more useful to introduce the idea of separate rooms for different functions. With this program it is very useful to go to, or see a video of, a real newspaper being produced.

The possibilities offered by a new program can be discussed with the class, and usually generate interest and enthusiasm. This creates opportunities for self-sponsored writing which, despite the advantages discussed by a number of writers (Graves, 1983; Calkins, 1986), can be difficult to arrange in many classes. Teachers organise word processing time in a number of ways. One way is to ask the children to form their own groups of three or more and decide what they want to use the program for. The group can then sign up on a large sheet of paper on the wall and await their turn. Each group writes the dates of their turns by their names on the list, and this helps the children to predict when their turn will come and allows the teacher to use the information for record keeping. It also makes it easy to pinpoint those children who do not sign up for one reason or another, so that the teacher can tackle this.

Peer tutoring

A class introduction generates interest, enthusiasm, talk and ideas but is not sufficient introduction to most programs. The effectiveness of peer tutoring has been discussed by Topping (1987) and the introduction of new programs seems to be a good area for this. Following the class discussion, a small group of children are chosen to be the class 'experts' for this program. These are not the particularly able children, but rather a mixture of those who usually avoid the computer, who lack confidence and those who show interest. Different children are chosen each time. They can be set a task using the program. The group might do some planning on paper, but compose straight on to the computer under the teacher's supervision. By the time they have completed their task they are familiar with the program and in a position to help other children in the class. This approach uses a large chunk of teacher time on a few children, and the rest of the class's work must be planned around this, but when the other groups start, they work with the advice of one of the 'experts' and teacher intervention is usually unnecessary. These 'experts' will work in turns with different groups, and this time seems to be well spent from both the learner's and tutor's point of view. This said, of course, some children will need advice about helping rather than interfering as they (like teachers) are inclined to pre-empt experimentation.

Planning, revising, and editing

These are processes that are fundamental to crafting writing and are used in varying degrees in most writing. The flexibility offered by the computer means that work which will be heavily redrafted is well suited to word processing. This should not cut out paper altogether as revising and editing may be done on a printed hard copy then transferred to the screen, either because of turn taking constraints or because some individuals prefer it this way.

Planning may be done on the computer, although this is time-consuming. It is probably best to encourage children to use paper for making brief notes and plans. Some will then make a rough draft on paper and transfer this to the screen when their turn comes. This is not ideal as most children cannot type to a copy typing speed and find it frustrating. Composing directly on to the screen seems to have much more to offer in terms of real sharing, useful discussion and decision making. At some point the group may need to revise or edit the work. It is important to distinguish between revising, which is a qualitative process concerned with composition, and editing, which is concerned with the transcription details. This distinction needs to be clear to the children. Authors should be encouraged to ask themselves questions about the appropriateness of their work, and teachers can help this through conferencing (Calkins, 1986). However teachers should not be the only source of criticism, and children must learn to assume the responsibility themselves. One way to start this is by using drafting cards as a guide for children. The revision side of the card contains five questions and a code to use on hard copy (Fig. 20.1). On the other side of the card is an editing code to use on hard copy (Fig. 20.2). Both sides of the card stress that the child should involve a friend.

Cut and paste

The electronic cut and paste feature of programs such as *Pendown* and *Typesetter* makes word processed work flexible in its presentation and encourages the authors to consider the needs of a reader. However, it can be difficult to introduce. The necessity for mov-

Figure 20.1

Content Editing

Go through the passage
carefully with a friend.
Read it aloud and
look at the text.

Consider: Does it make
              sense?

              Is it
              interesting?

              Is it a good
              Length?

              Does it start and
              end well?

              Is anything
              missing?

[   ]   Is this bit
              necessary?

(   )   Needs changing?
              Something left
              out.

～～～ ?   I don't quite
              understand.

Figure 20.2

<u>Copy Editing</u>

Go carefully through the work with a friend.

Read it aloud.

∧   Word or letters left out.

O   Punctuation mark missing or in the wrong place.

SP   Spelling error

\   Space missing

O^c   Capital letter in the wrong place.

ing text on screen can be abstract to children until they have tried physical cut and paste themselves and it would be beneficial for all classes to try making up a sheet physically. This will give them a concrete introduction to the process on screen.

Larger projects

Having involved children in group work on the word processor, many teachers will go on to use it for a class task such as a guide book, newspaper or annual. *Typesetter* is especially suitable for this purpose.

When planning a larger project it is important that the children have a certain degree of control, and are as involved to the fullest extent possible (Wray, 1985), and this means that the teacher must organise carefully. When groups sign up for larger projects and state what part they wish to do, the teacher will need to do some negotiating.

As part of a larger project the team of 'experts' (children familiar with the computer program) can also be editors of the finished product and select the stories, artwork, etc that will appear in the final version.

Physically it is easier to manage a large publication on the word processor if it is organised around an editor's desk holding the computer and all the interviews, tapes, plans, drafts and discs used. These can be organised in deep trays and divided by task sheets (Fig. 20.3) so that the teacher can see at a glance how work is progressing.

Passing it on

When a group of 'experts' have worked with a program for some time they can assemble a few lines about it for the next class, or change the notes they received with the program. It is surprising how easily young juniors can achieve this. In one case the children gradually produced a map of *Typesetter* and then presented the final copy using the program (Wray and Medwell, 1989). This was a useful experience which also helped the next class.